Ashes, Glory, Spirit

Ashes, Glory, Spirit

Daily Meditations for Lent, Easter Season, and Pentecost

by
Peter A. Chiara

Saint Mary's Press
Christian Brothers Publications
Winona, Minnesota

I would like to dedicate these reflections to my beloved parents, Rosalia and Gaspare Chiara, my dear sister, Antoinette, and my brothers, Nick, Joey, and Nicky, who created an atmosphere in which the initial seed of God's grace could come to birth within me.

The publishing team included Carl Koch, development editor; Rebecca Fairbank, copy editor; James H. Gurley, production editor; Hollace Storkel, typesetter; Cindi Ramm, cover designer; pre-press, printing, and binding by the graphics division of Saint Mary's Press.

The Scripture quotations that begin each meditation are from the New American Bible. Copyright © 1970 by the Confraternity of Christian Doctrine, 3211 Fourth Street NE, Washington, DC 20017. All rights reserved.

All other scriptural quotations herein are from the New Revised Standard Version of the Bible. Copyright © 1989 by the Division of Christian Education of the National Council of the Churches of Christ in the United States of America. All rights reserved.

Printed in the United States of America

Printing: 9 8 7 6 5 4 3 2 1

Year: 2008 07 06 05 04 03 02 01 00

ISBN 0-88489-619-6

 Genuine recycled paper with 10% post-consumer waste. Printed with soy-based ink.

Contents

Preface

In 1963, Pope John XXIII died. It was reported that when he was dying, those who were close to him could hear him say, *"Unum sins,"* "That they may be one." At the Last Supper, Jesus prayed the same words. Not only did Jesus pray that we might become one, but he made those words the basic proof for others to believe that he is the One sent by God to show God's infinite love for us.

These daily meditations for Lent, Easter season, and Pentecost are offered to stir within our hearts a renewed desire for unity and community. The most basic and fundamental teaching of Vatican Council II was our need for community. Until that time, Catholics had accepted individualism as the norm. The privatizing of our faith was readily preached from the pulpits, and "saving my soul" and private devotions and even private administering of the sacraments were the order of the day. It is my firm conviction that if we can lift our awareness of what Jesus has done to us and for us, our own goodness and sincerity will inspire us to make practical applications of God's word both to our life and to the life of the church and society.

I had intended to title these reflections *Garlic and Oil Christians* in the hope that they would encourage us to live our ordinary lives in a more Christian manner, thus bringing out the best in us. When we sauté our vegetables in garlic and oil, we notice a flavorful difference in their taste. The oil soothes, smooths, and, above all, penetrates to make the food gently surrender to the heat. The garlic definitely brings the food to another level. Garlic is like love, "when you got it, you got it" and everyone knows you "got it."

Christians should make a big difference in the life of the world. We, the people of God, should surrender day in and day out to the gentle, pervasive warmth of the Spirit's love. This love has brought us to another level; we share divinity with the Trinity. As far back as the writing of the psalms, the Chosen People spoke of the "odor of sanctity" to proclaim their uniqueness in God's eyes.

We are a eucharistic people. For most of us, Sunday liturgy is a time for togetherness. How can we sustain ourselves as a eucharistic community? One of the most effective ways is by praying the word of God in the daily liturgy. The church itself is the most basic sacrament, enabling us to live our daily life in Christ. The command to go forth to all nations is given to the church. Particular saints are a joy, but it is the church that produces them. It is the church that must constantly proclaim the Reign of God and reflect on the culture of its time.

The three great constitutions proclaimed by the Second Vatican Council were designed to remind us of our identity as church. *The Constitution on the Church* answered the question What is the church? We are a people. *The Constitution on the Liturgy* proclaimed that our lives were celebration. *The Constitution on the Modern World* declared that we were to live in the world, but not to be of the world.

A fractured church, like a fractured body, is limited and crippled. By lifting the awareness of who we are, we become more available to the Holy Spirit as sacraments "to be one as Jesus and the Father are one."

How to Use These Meditations

1. Place yourself in the presence of God. Then slowly repeat two or three times a line from the Scriptures that will quiet your mind and heart: for instance, "Be still, and know that I am God!" (Psalm 46:10).

2. If possible, slowly read the epistle, responsorial psalm, and Gospel for the liturgy of the day from a missal or missalette.
3. Read the passage from the daily readings that begins each day's meditation. Indeed, read it several times, letting its meanings take hold of your spirit. If possible, read the passage aloud.
4. Read and ponder the two-paragraph reflection on the passage.
5. Offer the short prayer. Add your own spontaneous prayer if you feel moved to do so.
6. Consider the reflection question. It is addressed to you. Carry it with you throughout the day.
7. Make a spiritual communion. Tell Jesus wholeheartedly how much you love him, and ask for the grace that it be done to you according to his Word. In your poverty and nakedness, let God enrich you, clothe you, and fashion you.

You must glorify God by being you and by enabling the Body of Christ—your uniqueness united to others'—to be more than it is. We can become transformed to become who we are and Whose we are by meditating on God's word, praying with it, and opening ourself to the spirit of God active within us.

Peter A. Chiara

Ash Wednesday

Blow the trumpet in Zion!

$\cdot \quad \cdot \quad \cdot \quad \cdot \quad \cdot \quad \cdot \quad \cdot$

> *call an assembly;*
> *Gather the people.*
>   *(Joel 2:15–16)*

If Joel were speaking to us today, he might say: "To the Body of Christ in America, I tell you: I know of bloodshed along the Mohawk River; of your suffering for me because you were immigrants; of your sacrifices to build parishes and schools to worship me and to protect the children; of the thousands of your children generously given to ministry, religious life, and the priesthood; of the high regard in which you have held marriage and family life.

"But I have this against you, that you have abandoned your First Love. Remember then from what you have fallen, repent, and do the works you did before (cf. Revelation 2:4). Come back to me with all your heart, as a bride adorned for her husband. Repent. Return to me."

Prayer. O God, set me on fire for you. Let me hunger and thirst to be what you want me to be.

Reflection. If at this moment I could be granted anything I desired, what would I ask for?

Thursday After Ash Wednesday

I have set before you life and death, the blessing and the curse. Choose life, then, that you and your descendants may live, by loving the Lord, your God. (Deuteronomy 30:19–20)

A key part of Christian spirituality has always been accepting God's will. When confronted with crosses—sudden death, unsuspected terminal illness, unexpected loss of employment—most of us try genuinely, even if painfully, to accept them as somehow part of God's will. We suffer patiently.

Even so, the cross of fidelity in the face of rejection, mockery, luxury, and success is not so readily a part of our life. The cross of removing ourselves from the center and giving Jesus and the Gospel the center is difficult. The temptation to rationalize the cross has a long history in the church. Moments after Peter proclaimed, "You are the Christ," he tried to convince Jesus to avoid the cross. Our first option is often not Jesus, but ourself. However, our faith offers us an admonition not to go too far in choosing the world lest we lose our soul. Jesus reminded Peter that God's ways are not our ways.

Prayer. Dear God, help me to be and to live as Jesus crucified.

Reflection. In what ways do I choose life as Jesus sees life?

Friday After Ash Wednesday

This, rather, is the fasting that I wish:
releasing those bound unjustly,
untying the thongs of the yoke;
Setting free the oppressed,
breaking every yoke.

(Isaiah 58:6)

Saint Paul compared the church to a body: "Now you are the body of Christ and individually members of it" (1 Corinthians 12:27). An essential and life-giving fast for Christ's Body, the church, would be a deep desire to be only what God wants us to be. The Body of Christ participates in healthy, holy fasting by freeing those bound by addiction, injustice, or oppression.

Re-examining our concepts of what we "give up" for Lent or how we fast could be a life-enhancing experience. To be a healthy Body of Christ, each of us must be ourself and not another, while at the same time joining together with all God's people in truth, justice, and charity. No one person is the Body of Christ. When we fast from our need for control over others, from our need for victory, we can join hands with our sisters and brothers as one Body of Christ.

Prayer. Loving God, may I be one with you as you and Jesus are one.

Reflection. Do I truly accept my responsibility beyond my immediate family for releasing those who are bound unjustly?

Saturday After Ash Wednesday

"Repairer of the breach," they shall call you.

. . . .

If you hold back your foot on the sabbath
from following your own pursuits on my holy day;

. . . .

Then you shall delight in the Lord.
(Isaiah 58:12–14)

Jesus said to them, "The healthy do not need a doctor, sick people do. I have not come to invite the self-righteous to a change of heart, but sinners." (Luke 5:31–32)

Sunday worship is essential to the life of the church. We not only celebrate God's unconditional love, we actually relive it. We re-enact the death and Resurrection of Jesus. If we are disposed in our heart to accepting this profound gift of Jesus, we grow to have his mind and will in us. We become like Jesus. Our heart gradually grows from a heart of stone to a heart of flesh, a heart dimly reflecting the sacred heart of Jesus.

The Christian community celebrates the Sabbath Eucharist to deepen itself in love. The poorest of poor people, the sickest of sick people are us sinners. Jesus came to heal us of sin; this is true evangelization. And at the heart of our healing is our Sabbath celebration of the Eucharist.

Prayer. Lord, rescue us from death and feed us in time of famine.

Reflection. How do I live the Sunday liturgy all week? Am I dying and rising in order to give life to others?

First Sunday of Lent (Year A)

And so man became a living being. *(Genesis 2:7)*

We trivialize Lent if we see it simply as giving up things rather than as giving up our false self. The first Sunday of Lent is the most challenging. We have to decide if we want to be fully alive and if we are willing to struggle with all the opposition that is an inevitable part of following Christ. Adam and Eve fell to temptation. Jesus was challenged by temptation. Indeed, God mercifully inspired the writer of Matthew's Gospel to include the scene of Jesus' temptation to show us that no one is exempt from the struggle to be fully alive.

Being fully alive does not come from some canonical or legalistic approval rating. It means living with the burning desire to love with our whole heart, soul, and mind. It implies offering our whole being to become one with God. The grace of Lent gives us a new opportunity to return to God, who is life.

Prayer. "Create in me a clean heart, O God, / and put a new and right spirit within me" (Psalm 51:10).

Reflection. What is the basic goal of my life?

First Sunday of Lent (Year B)

This is the time of fulfillment. The reign of God is at hand!
Reform your lives and believe in the good news! (Mark
1:15)

ℐ This incredible announcement came after Jesus spent forty
days in prayer and fasting, listening to the Spirit. Absolutely
shocking! It was the proclamation of a spiritual revolution: "The
moment you have been waiting for is here. The working out of the
details for the next two and a half years will cause pain, anger, joy,
division, scandal, murder on Calvary, and ultimately an astonishing
Resurrection to life on Easter. But for now, hear this, 'the Reign of
God is here.'"

Lent is primarily about Baptism, that is, about accepting divine
grace to be God's child, to share divine life, to be part of God's body,
the church. It is a gratuitous gift from God. Lenten reform, or bap-
tismal grace, is not primarily a question of morality. It is first a fact
of being and believing who we are, and then a question of how we
will respond. Lent is our yearly desert time to remind ourself that
Jesus makes a difference. Our God rules.

Prayer. God, all I want is to know Christ, to share Christ's
suffering and the power of Christ's love.

Reflection. Do I truly believe that the coming of Jesus is an
entirely new way of looking at life?

First Sunday of Lent (Year C)

*When the devil had finished all this tempting he left him
[Jesus], to await another opportunity. (Luke 4:13)*

G3 The Gospel message is the story of how to become fully
human in resurrected life. The fundamental event is Christ
raised to life. This completion of the mission of Jesus opens the
possibility of hope for peace here and hereafter.

The story of Jesus' temptation highlights what most deters us
from accepting resurrected life: fear coming from insecurity. We
want to have our bread, our power, our angelic protection from
harm or death. Jesus turned away from these temptations, knowing
that the life God gave him was enough. The Reign of God is about
peace, love, and justice, not scraps of food, political power, or
testing God. Jesus is our hope of glory, not an exception from living.
So temptations will come again and again until we pass to the next
life. The paschal mystery of daily dying and rising is the path to
genuine humanity and union with God and others.

Prayer. "Ascribe to the Lord glory and strength" (Psalm 29:1).

Reflection. Can I name some persons in my life whom I
regard as truly human?

Monday
of the First Week of Lent

*You shall love your neighbor as yourself. I am the Lord.
(Leviticus 19:18)*

*I assure you, as often as you did it for one of my least
brothers, you did it for me. (Matthew 25:40)*

Every so often we hear the joke about marriage or other
relationships: "You and I are one, and I am the one." With
Jesus, matters are definitely different. Each of us is the one, with
him and with one another. So much does Jesus identify with us that
to neglect or to offend our brothers and sisters is to offend him. He
takes it personally. If we are in need—poor, hungry, imprisoned,
sick—he feels unloved.

Christian morality is much more than observing precepts. It is
the acceptance of the law of love in the Reign of God. The second
commandment, "love one another as I have loved you," is the
equivalent of the first commandment to love God with our whole
heart, mind, and soul. Love of neighbor is the only concrete proof
of faithfulness to the first commandment. Nothing is easier to say
than "I love God." The proof is in the pudding.

Prayer. Holy Spirit of love, help me to see you in myself and
in others.

Reflection. How can I love God, whom I cannot see, if I do
not love others whom I can see?

Tuesday
of the First Week of Lent

This is how you are to pray:
"Our Father . . ."
(Matthew 6:8)

One of the most consoling revelations of Jesus' spiritual revolution is the truth of God as Father. Elsewhere in the Scriptures, Jesus uses the word *Abba,* meaning "Pappa" or "Daddy." Jesus himself was constantly seeking his Pappa's will, his Dad's help, his Father's blessing. He was sent by his Abba to save us from sin and death.

A good parent is one who knows us, loves us, and assists us. Many of our parents know us and love us but are powerless to help us. Many have knowledge and power but lack love. Others have love but do not know our deepest needs. Only our heavenly Parent can truly give us life:

So shall my word be that goes from my mouth;
    it shall not return to me empty,
but it shall accomplish that which I purpose,
    and succeed in the thing for which I sent it.

(Isaiah 55:11)

As God's people, we should constantly hallow God's name, seek God's will, and ask for God's life-giving bread and healing mercy.

Prayer. Our Father, our Pappa, our Dad.

Reflection. Do I live with the conviction of God's unconditional love for me?

19

Wednesday
of the First Week of Lent

A broken, humbled heart,
O God, you will not scorn.
(Psalm 51:19)

None of us likes to be dependent: "Don't worry, she can take care of herself"; "he has it all together, he will be okay." These phrases are signs of praise and security often cited about people facing some crisis. They can be words of pride or words of humility. If they speak of our own strength, such pride can keep us closed off from God's grace and from other people. No one or nothing is needed, not even God. Sometimes we have so much power, health, success, or even "the one true faith" that we are blind to our limitations and our lack of love for others.

On the other hand, if our strength comes from our weakness, we will be open and grateful to God for the gifts in our life. Our honest admission of sin, coupled with our deep desire to be truly ourself and to share in the Body of Christ, will make us open to our need for God's care.

Prayer. "O that today you would listen to his voice! / Do not harden your hearts" (Psalm 95:7–8).

Reflection. How has my own sin blinded me from experiencing God working in my life?

Thursday
of the First Week of Lent

*My Lord, our King, you alone are God. Help me, who am
alone and have no help but you, for I am taking my life in
my hand. (Esther C 12:14–15)*

This prayer speaks of courage, trust, and love. In God's
unconditional love for us, God entrusted us with the work
of salvation for all. As the Body of Christ, we are to enter into the
battle against evil to see that our God reigns in our heart and in the
world.

We might be tempted to say, "What can I do? I'm only one
person and I have no power and few gifts, none of which is particu-
larly outstanding." This is when we must hear the words of Jesus,
"O you of little faith." This is our Savior, who took a few loaves and
fish joyfully and generously offered by a child and fed five thousand. He tells us that no parents would hand their children a stone
if they asked for bread. How much more will Jesus give us than
these earthly parents if we but ask? We must accept our responsibility as part of the Body of Christ, no matter how small, and ask
our loving God to help us be a life-giving member of a life-giving
community.

Prayer. Ask and you will receive, seek and you will find,
knock and the door will be opened.

Reflection. In my relationship with Jesus, which is the most
dominant: the quality of my faith, hope, and love or the quality of
my power—how much I possess?

Friday of the First Week of Lent

Do I indeed derive any pleasure from the death of the wicked? says the Lord God. Do I not rather rejoice when he turns from his evil way that he may live? (Ezekiel 18:23)

To be a life-giving member of the community, we must realize two basic dispositions: first, true spirituality is a conversion of the heart and not an external fidelity or loyalty to juridical precepts. In a previous generation, it was possible never to eat meat on Friday and yet to be a glutton. It was possible to never miss Mass on Sunday and yet to never grow in holiness. We must give God our heart, love for Love.

Second, our interior conversion must be constantly sought. The church, as a wise mother, gives us this holy season to remind us that no matter what level of commitment we have reached, we must constantly grow in our love of God. The virtues of the past will not be collateral for the sins of the present. Now is the acceptable moment.

Prayer. "I wait for the LORD, my soul waits, / and in his word I hope" (Psalm 130:5).

Reflection. Is my love true love if I set limits on it?

Saturday
of the First Week of Lent

I will give you thanks with an upright heart,
when I have learned your just ordinances.
(Psalm 119:7)

In unconditional love, God has slowly and carefully prepared a number of covenants with us and made promises
to us, calling us the chosen people. After the Flood, God promised
Noah with the bow in the clouds that never again would people be
so punished. To Moses, Yahweh gave the Ten Commandments as
the standard of our response to that particular Covenant. God has
Jeremiah proclaim that the law of love will be written on our hearts.

The new Covenant of love enables us to share in the divine life
of God, initially in the sacrament of Baptism, and in an ongoing
way, through the eucharistic love of God and our neighbor. The
terms of this Covenant are radically different: Jesus says, "Love
your enemies and pray for those who persecute you" (cf. Matthew
5:43–48). We are the Body of Christ called to love all people, not
just those who love us. This is the new ordinance and Covenant.

Prayer. "God so loved the world that he gave his only Son, so
that everyone who believes in him may not perish but have eternal
life" (John 3:16).

Reflection. Is my desire for God as strong as God's desire for
me?

Second Sunday of Lent (Year A)

The Lord said to Abram: "Go forth from the land of your kinsfolk and from your father's house to a land that I will show you." (Genesis 12:1)

Moses as the lawgiver and Elijah as the prophet were the key persons calling the descendants of Abram to be God's people. Israel had a unique relationship and moral code with Yahweh. Jesus is the new Moses, the new prophet.

The Apostles, as key members of the new People of God, were to model God's Reign for all. In today's Gospel, three Apostles experience Jesus' Transfiguration, but the real transfiguration consists in their new awareness that Jesus is the Messiah. They, especially Peter, wanted to stop everything and rest in this glorious moment. But Jesus declared that they had to take up their cross for the new life in Christ and their eternal transfiguration. Yes, Jesus is the Messiah, but first he had to die and rise. So the church takes up its cross daily, constantly reflecting on the signs of the times and guiding its members to an authentic Christlike response.

Prayer. "The LORD has done great things for us, / and we rejoiced" (Psalm 126:3).

Reflection. What does the new law and prophetic stance in Christ mean to me?

Second Sunday of Lent (Year B)

This is my Son, my beloved. Listen to him. (Mark 9:7)

A few years ago, while preparing a couple for marriage, I was confronted by a strange reply to the prenuptial inquiry form. In answer to the question "Do you commit yourself to an indissoluble union," the young man replied, "No." He was the child of an army officer. He had moved many times, attended several schools, earned two masters' degrees. He said: "Permanent commitment is almost impossible in a dynamic culture like ours. There are too many demands if you are really alive." Unlike this young man, Peter wanted to capture the moment of Jesus' Transfiguration by erecting structures on the site. He wanted things to stay as they were.

Neither response will give true life here and now. To be static and possessive is to die. To follow every impulse is to be rootless, superficial. The love of God demands love in return. Love is not static, but neither can it be blown away by the slightest wind. We should not be afraid to love. The suffering that inevitably comes from wholehearted love is the purifying of self that will fashion us in the image of God.

Prayer. Gracious God, teach me that to love is to be human, to be fully alive, to rise from death, to reach the top of the mountain.

Reflection. Am I open to being led to the wholehearted love that continually forms me in God's image?

Second Sunday of Lent (Year C)

Jesus took Peter, John and James, and went up onto a mountain to pray. (Luke 9:28)

J Luke gives prayer as the motive for Jesus' going to the mountain. Jesus has set his course to go to Jerusalem to suffer and die. He now takes Peter, James, and John apart so that they will be with him as he speaks to God for guidance and strength for the struggle. Like any leader challenging the status quo, he has presentiments about his approaching death and about the challenges his followers will face.

Jesus' prayer is one of detachment and unconditional surrender to the spirit of God. Having thus emptied himself of everything, the glory of God manifests itself externally from his interior union with God. Moses and Elijah also appear "in glory" (Luke 9:31). So will it be for us. "He will transform the body of our humiliation that it may be conformed to the body of his glory" (Philippians 3:21).

Prayer. "Hear, O LORD, when I cry aloud, / be gracious to me and answer me!" (Psalm 27:7).

Reflection. Have Christian prayer and openness to God's will any genuine role in my lifestyle?

Monday
of the Second Week of Lent

Be compassionate as your Father is compassionate. (Luke 6:36)

℘ Perhaps no other demand of Jesus identifies our new life in Christ as much as the challenge of compassion. The word *compassion* is rooted in Latin to mean "suffer with." The word *sympathy* is the same, having its roots in Greek. This passage reminds us that we are called to be so united with God and one another that we should feel what God feels for our sisters and brothers, especially for those killing themselves by sin and selfishness.

The power of our love expressed by not judging or condemning others may be their only hope: love "rejoices in the truth. It bears all things, believes all things, hopes all things, endures all things" (1 Corinthians 13:6–7). Like Jesus, the head of the Body, every member should be committed to the health of the whole Body of Christ, especially God's poor people, sinful people, sick people.

Prayer. Holy One, help me not to seek "my own advantage, but that of many, so that they may be saved" (1 Corinthians 10:33).

Reflection. *"Mi casa es su casa,"* or "My house is your house," might also be phrased: Your pain, suffering, and fear are my pain, suffering, and fear. Can I say, *"mi casa es su casa"*?

Tuesday
of the Second Week of Lent

All their works are performed to be seen. *(Matthew 23:5)*

Whether in the church or in society, a title or position of authority places us in danger of believing that we are more than we are. The danger is even greater when titles, either ecclesiastical or civil, are bestowed and are purely honorary. Institutions and bureaucracies spawn shallowness.

The church has been around for a very long time, and it has spawned its own share of superficialities. This holy season could be the time for honest appraisal of our role in the church, either by self-examination or by questioning others. The answer might resemble the child in the fairy tale of the emperor's clothes: "Mommy, look, the King has no clothes on." It might not be as bad as it sounds. After all, we do follow a crucified, naked King.

Prayer. Creator of the universe, let me not think of myself as either great or small. Let my works be done for the good of your people.

Reflection. Is my self-worth based on God's love for me or on my desire for recognition?

Wednesday
of the Second Week of Lent

The Son of Man . . . has come, not to be served by others but to serve, to give his own life as a ransom for the many. (Matthew 20:28)

Today's readings reveal the dimensions of the spiritual revolution brought by Jesus. Quite innocently, but boldly, the mother of James and John attempts to establish her children in key positions in the Reign of God. Jesus will have none of it. The Kingdom is not of this world, nor is it established by power and might. The Reign of God is a reign of love in which the rulers are to serve, not to be served. The rulers are the servants.

The quality of the service is life itself. We begin to see signs of the intensity of the struggle to free us from sin and death. To make it possible for us to be fully human, Jesus drank of the cup of self-emptying love. The struggle goes on in each of us. It is the power of the Spirit in the community of self-emptying love that combats evil and fosters life.

Prayer. My God, help me to drink of the cup of self-emptying love that Jesus drank.

Reflection. How is my own love self-emptying and total?

Thursday
of the Second Week of Lent

They will not be convinced even if one should rise from the dead. (Luke 16:31)

Lent is a good time to check whether we have grown more open to life or more isolated. What are we living for? What is our focus? Perhaps we are so content and comfortable that we do not feel a strong need for God or anyone else.

In Luke's story for today, the rich man, Dives, never really "saw" the beggar Lazarus. Dives just passed him by. For us, maybe viewing genocide, famine, and massive destruction on television has hardened our heart and deadened our compassion. Lent is a good time to start "seeing" again, even if what we see wrenches our heart and shatters our complacency. When we open our eyes and heart and hands in service, the Body of Christ can exhibit the compassion of Jesus in creative and exciting ways. Then we will be living the resurrected life of Christ.

Prayer. Compassionate God, deepen my faith. Help me to believe that I no longer live, but you live in me with all your power to free me from death and indifference.

Reflection. If I am blinded by what is going on around me, how can I be helped to see?

Friday
of the Second Week of Lent

Reuben . . . tried to save [Joseph] . . . saying, "We must not take his life." . . . Judah said to his brothers, "What is to be gained by killing our brother?" (Genesis 37:21,26)

So often we hear of evil people who have a "soft spot" in their heart for a favorite child or a dearly beloved friend. Their hands have been bloodied by murder, abuse, or torture of others, but they too manifest a soft spot of love or tenderness. Could this soft spot not be a faint glimmer of the divine image in each of us, hidden under years of sinfulness?

Thérèse of Lisieux, the Little Flower, seemed to specialize in offering herself and her prayer for condemned criminals, lest they be hanged spiritually dead. Did not the dying, crucified Jesus get through to the heart of the Good Thief? Prayer, fasting, and alms-giving are mighty weapons in the hands of the loving community.

Prayer. Holy One, hear my voice when I call to you. Do not desert me, my Savior, my God.

Reflection. How do I see the connection between love and life?

Saturday
of the Second Week of Lent

I will break away and return to my father. (Luke 15:18)

When the deputation of followers of John the Baptist asked Jesus who he was, Jesus replied that they should go back and tell John what they saw and heard: the Good News was being preached to poor people, and lame people were being cured. When Jesus was asked how many times they should forgive, Peter was shocked to hear seventy times seven. Indeed, the great scandal of Jesus' teaching is the unconditional mercy of God. It offends our human sense of justice. The story of the prodigal son is another story of mercy, this time about a prodigal father. What else could a real father do but throw a party? His son was dead and has returned.

During this holy season, it is good to remind ourselves of our Baptism. God loves us totally. We are God's beloved children. Nothing can diminish God's love for us and God's willingness to wait for eternity for us to come home.

Prayer. Merciful God, help me to realize more deeply who I am and Whose I am.

Reflection. Does my conviction of God's unconditional love lead me to presumption and arrogance, or does it lead me to reverence and respect?

Third Sunday of Lent (Year A)

God is Spirit,
and those who worship him
must worship in Spirit and truth.
(John 4:24)

Certainly, in speaking to the Samaritan woman, the incarnate God wasn't trying to remove the symbols from faith, though he was warning her that the time would come when the place where people worshiped would cease to matter (cf. John 4:23). Actually, Jesus wanted her to understand that faith is an interior disposition of the heart that transcends time, place, and objects.

Too often we conduct rituals and receive sacraments that fail to deepen our relationship with Jesus. The sacraments are channels of grace, but we need to be prepared to receive God's love. Lent is a time to worship in Spirit and in truth, not just in external practices.

Prayer. O God, be mindful of my indifference and cold routine. Teach me to be in communion with you.

Reflection. How can I grow in awareness of the power and beauty of encountering Jesus in the sacraments?

Third Sunday of Lent (Year B)

Get them out of here! Stop turning my Father's house into a marketplace! (John 2:16)

Perhaps one of the most frightening episodes in the New Testament is Jesus expelling the money changers from the Temple. He is thoroughly outraged! Using religious purity as an excuse for making a profit, the money changers charged an exorbitant price. This even prevented some people from offering worship. In addition, for centuries, the prophets cried out against animal sacrifices offered without interior devotion and gratitude.

When challenged about where he got the authority to do what he did, Jesus proclaimed: "Destroy this temple, and in three days I will raise it up" (John 2:19). Years later, John the Evangelist realized that the Resurrection fulfilled this messianic claim. The new Temple, the risen Christ, will be available to all, in every place and time, not dependent on human structures. Thus we will worship in "spirit and truth" (John 4:24).

Prayer.

The law of the LORD is perfect,
    reviving the soul;
the decrees of the LORD are sure,
    making wise the simple.
                              (Psalm 19:7)

Reflection. When churches and lavish appointments are used as substitutes for true devotions, they are offensive to God. How about to me?

Third Sunday of Lent (Year C)

Then perhaps it will bear fruit. If not, it shall be cut down.
(Luke 13:9)

We hear on television and read in newspapers of terrible atrocities and crimes. We might be tempted to say we are not like those sinners. Perhaps because we are not so bad, we feel we are fairly good. As Christians, we believe that the God of life, "I am who am," has freed us. We also believe that God has given us spirit and food and drink for our journey through the desert.

Yet too many of us are like the fig tree; we produce little or no fruit. We live by the "serious sin, little sin" game. We measure our response to God and weigh our offenses, usually giving ourself the best measure. We feel no genuine need for repentance; we simply are not that bad. Well, Lent is a good time to take stock of the fruit we have borne.

Prayer. "Lord, help me to love and not count the cost" (Saint Ignatius).

Reflection. To whom much is given, much is expected.

Monday
of the Third Week of Lent

No prophet gains acceptance in his native place. (Luke 4:24)

God is so transcendent that for some of us the idea of a God incarnate is blasphemy. Or we may readily profess Jesus, God taking on flesh, but at the same time, the idea of truly imitating him is out of the question. The invisible God is visible in Jesus, and now we, the church, the people of God, make God visible.

Does our manner of living either personally or as a Christian community say anything about who we are? Do I have to wear a particular cross or medal or go to a parish church to be known as a Christian? Have I ever been the voice for the voiceless poor or let anyone's pain touch me? Am I quick to dismiss with quick clichés those who are prophetic voices?

Prayer. Dear God, if today I hear your voice, let me not harden my heart, even if the prophet is a poor person or an enemy.

Reflection. How seriously do I take the responsibility of being the visible sign of Jesus in the world?

Tuesday
of the Third Week of Lent

Let our sacrifice be in your presence today
as we follow you unreservedly.
(Daniel 3:40)

Jesus came to give life and to give it abundantly. Jesus is truly human, and Christians define humanity in terms of who he is and not who we are. At the core of his humanity is mercy. Giving mercy unreservedly is the sacrifice God desires because it is the sacrifice God offers us every day: forgiveness of our offenses. So we forgive those who have offended us because God has forgiven us first out of love.

Mercy, more than anything else, releases us from death and inhumanity. During Lent, then, we pray for the creative power of the Holy Spirit, the potter, to fashion us to the image and likeness of the incarnate God. Mercy softens the heart of stone and makes it pliable in God's hands.

Prayer. God, the potter, take my heart of stone and make it a heart of flesh, a sacred heart.

Reflection. Do I pick and choose to whom and when I should show mercy?

Wednesday
of the Third Week of Lent

Whoever fulfills and teaches these commands shall be great in the kingdom of God. (Matthew 5:19)

Both in Deuteronomy (4:5–9) and in Matthew's Gospel (5:19), the Scriptures praise those who remember God's ways and pass them on to others. It is not, however, an academic learning that Jesus praises. Formal teaching and learning are great gifts for those to whom they are given. The holy word is among our greatest treasures, but here both Moses and the new Moses—Jesus—are telling us that *we* are the message.

Through prayer, the word of God must become the fabric of our life. We must become the word of God and spread Christ's message by who we are, the Body of Christ. The good tree bears good fruit, and the bad tree bears bad fruit. The creative power of God in Christ is released through us when we make his word our own. We live in every word that comes forth from the mouth of God.

Prayer. O God, "show me the path of life. / In your presence there is fullness of joy" (Psalm 16:11).

Reflection. God is love. I am made in the image and likeness of God, therefore, I must be love.

Thursday
of the Third Week of Lent

The man who is not with me is against me. The man who does not gather with me scatters. (Luke 11:23)

Today is the midpoint of Lent. In ancient times, when Lenten penitential practices were much more severe, the day had a joyful and encouraging tone so that people would not become discouraged. We might observe today as a day to pray for our sisters and brothers who are indifferent, and for ourselves lest we become indifferent.

The greatest danger to the Body of Christ is indifferent members. We can clearly name our enemies and take precautions against the wolves in sheeps' clothing. The indifferent are more difficult to identify. They are in the Body, but definitely not part of the Body. Their presence poisons the atmosphere of wholehearted commitment to the life of the church and its mission. Not to make a decision for Christ is already a decision against him.

Prayer. Come, Holy Spirit, enkindle in me the fire of your love.

Reflection. To do nothing is to be nothing. At the midpoint of Lent, how am I doing?

Friday of the Third Week of Lent

I am like a verdant cypress tree—
Because of me you will bear fruit!
(Hosea 14:9)

We are three weeks away from Good Friday, the day when on the verdant cypress tree of the cross, we will be the fruit of God's love. Our crucified and risen brother, Jesus, has paid the price and washed us clean in his blood.

It remains for us to continually surrender to his love and allow him to make us in his image and likeness. "God is love" (cf. 1 John 4:16). If we are to be truly like Christ, we must not only practice love but also become love. The very essence of the Trinity is love begetting love and returning love. This is our incomprehensible destiny, to live the life of divine love now and forever.

Prayer. God, who is love, teach me to live that I may become love.

Reflection. Is my life an expression of redeeming love and the need to be continually redeemed?

Saturday
of the Third Week of Lent

Everyone who exalts himself shall be humbled while he who humbles himself shall be exalted. (*Luke 4:14*)

There is a Trinity of Love—Creator, Redeemer, and Sanctifier—pouring out an energy of creative love. There is also a trinity of self-righteousness—me, myself, and I—pouring out an energy of death. The Trinity of Love produces Jesus and the Mystical Body of Christ. The trinity of self-righteousness produces evil and a mystical body of conspiracy. The Trinity of Love creates unity, peace, and harmony. The trinity of self-righteousness produces disunity, war, and violence. The Trinity of Love produces compassion, forgiveness, and chastity. The trinity of self-righteousness produces individualism, hardness of heart, and abuse of self and others.

The Trinity of Love is the light that has come into the world. The trinity of self-righteousness is the blind leading the blind to utter darkness. The Trinity of Love leads to humanity; the trinity of self-righteousness to inhumanity. The good tree bears good fruit; the bad tree bears bad fruit.

Prayer. Create a clean heart in me, O God, and give back to me the joy of your salvation.

Reflection. Am I empowered by a relationship with the Trinity of Love or the trinity of self-righteousness?

Fourth Sunday of Lent (Year A)

"Do you believe in the Son of Man?" He answered, "Who is he, sir, that I may believe in him?" "You have seen him," Jesus replied. "He is speaking to you now." (John 9:35–37)

Today is Laetare Sunday, the day of anticipating and celebrating the victory of Jesus over sin and death. As we assemble as the Body of Christ, Jesus invites us to fill our heart with faith, hope, and love. Faith in Jesus is the power that will overcome the world. Hope is ours if we believe that the victory will be ours if we want it. Love is given to us because the victory is achieved by God's unconditional love.

It is not yet Easter, but joy cannot be contained. As we lift the cup in the eucharistic celebration, we know that victory is ours. No one given to the Spirit by our God will be lost, only the one who chooses to be lost.

Prayer. Your words, O God, are spirit and life for "you have the words of eternal life" (John 6:69).

Reflection. Do I really get a kick out of being a follower of Jesus? Is it a real joy for me?

Fourth Sunday of Lent (Year B)

God loved the world so much, he gave us his only Son.
(John 3:16)

The theme of light is prevalent in both the Old and New Testaments. In Exodus 13:21, God "went in front of them . . . in a pillar of fire by night, to give them light." Jesus is called "the light of all people" (John 1:4). In the sacrament of Baptism, the parents and godparents are given a lighted candle as these words are spoken: "Receive the light of Christ." This child must live as a child of light and never as a child of darkness.

To receive eternal life, our behavior must be characterized by daily fidelity to the risen life of Jesus within us. Our faith grows by our being faithful to Jesus. The Reign of God is already present in him and the victory over darkness already achieved. Through Baptism, the Reign of God is in us, and the victory will be ours here and hereafter by living in the light of Christ's words and actions.

Prayer. "The LORD is my light and my salvation" (Psalm 27:1).

Reflection. How can I grow from a state of mere religiosity to an adult Christian faith?

Fourth Sunday of Lent (Year C)

His father caught sight of him and . . . he ran out to meet him. (Luke 15:20)

The story of the prodigal son is definitely one of the best known in the New Testament. The young son asks for his share of his inheritance while his father is still alive. He uses it shamefully and is reduced to working in a pig sty. With less than noble motives, feeling sorry for himself and his painful condition, the son decides to go home and ask his father for a job. His father sights him way off in the distance, and here we see God at the divine best. The father runs to meet the boy and doesn't even give him a chance to recite his well-prepared act of contrition. He throws his arms around him, kisses him, has him clothed with a robe of gladness, and even throws a party. The older son hears the music and angrily refuses to enter the house. The father goes out to meet him but is rebuffed by self-righteous defense.

God is always running toward us, good, bad, or indifferent. It is God's love that should motivate us to conversion, to our return.

Prayer. O God, how could I ever forget your love!

Reflection. What is more important, my confession or God's mercy?

Monday
of the Fourth Week of Lent

*Lo, I am about to create new heavens
and a new earth.*
(Isaiah 65:17)

The joy of Laetare Sunday spills over to us today. The story of Jesus healing should give us joy and hope. The joy of the promises of a new heaven and a new earth has a Christmas ring to it. Jesus truly is Emmanuel, God-with-us. He responds to our need. In the Gospel, the centurion is a heartbroken father crushed at the thought of losing his son. But he "believed the word that Jesus spoke to him" (John 4:50), and his son was joyfully healed.

The best and only way to approach God is directly, like the centurion. Tell God, "I love you, and I need you." By abandoning ourselves to God's unconditional love, we invite God to make us new persons. When we accept that we mean as much to Jesus as he does to his Abba, God unleashes creative power to form us into the holy likeness in peace and joy.

Prayer. O God, "you have turned my mourning into dancing / . . . and clothed me with joy" (Psalm 30:11).

Reflection. In the face of hardship, even death, do I continue to rejoice in my Creator and Redeemer?

Tuesday
of the Fourth Week of Lent

I don't have anyone to plunge me into the pool once the water has been stirred up. (John 5:7)

Our Christian initiation begins at Baptism. We are washed clean in the living water of grace. The Holy Spirit begins fashioning us in the image and likeness of God. The Spirit overshadows us, and we are reborn as the children of God and members of the Body of Christ. We have someone to plunge us into the healing water: the Holy Spirit and our community.

However, the inner life of faith is not automatic. It demands a free response from a thirsty heart. If we want water from a faucet, we have to turn it on. If we want the Living Water of Baptism to continue to flow in our life and help us to grow in the life of Jesus, we must repeatedly turn our life around by constant conversion, a steady returning. All our choices create growth or stagnation. Choose life.

Prayer. O God, you are my refuge and my strength, my ever present help.

Reflection. What specific gifts do I have to give to others, and am I willing to use them?

Wednesday
of the Fourth Week of Lent

In a time of favor I answer you,
on the day of salvation I help you.
(Isaiah 49:8)

Today's readings are supportive and encouraging. God is with us on our journey to authentic wholeness. In the ancient church, the priest would put salt, the symbol of wisdom, on the tongue of the catechumens. They also received the Creed, the Lord's Prayer, and the four Gospels. Through prayer and reflection, they were making these truths their own. By gradually living these truths, they were to attain wisdom in a union of love.

In this liturgy, John reveals something of the relationship between the Son and the Father. For "the Father loves the Son and shows him all that he himself is doing" (John 5:20). We are in Christ and through him in the Father by the creative power of the Spirit. This trinitarian union is our strength, our joy, and our hope in our hunger and thirst for love.

Prayer. Lead, O kindly Light, you are just and kind in all your works (cf. Psalm 145:17).

Reflection. Do I take time regularly to reflect on the intensity and intimacy of God's love for me?

Thursday
of the Fourth Week of Lent

Search the Scriptures
in which you think if you have eternal life—
they also testify on my behalf.

(John 5:39)

Faith is the capacity to receive God in our heart. It implies setting our heart on God and being open to being changed, to becoming more than we are. We are being invited into the realm of mystery, not the realm of problem solving. Knowledge, understanding, and wisdom can help expand our faith and its implications, but arguing theology for the sake of victory rather than truth is a darkening hindrance.

Lent is a time to gently ponder the Scriptures, the words and actions of Jesus. It is a time to simply and silently place ourselves in the presence of God. Seeking Christ as the light of truth can lead to a profound communion of mind and heart with him, others, and all creation.

Prayer. God, that I may see!

Reflection. Do I envision faith as a static, unchanging relationship with God characterized by loyalty, or do I see it as a journey of changing intimacy in my relationship with God and others?

Friday
of the Fourth Week of Lent

To us he [the just one] is the censure of our thoughts;
merely to see him is a hardship for us,
Because his life is not like other men's,
and different are his ways.

(Wisdom 2:14–15)

"Show me your companions and I will show you what you are" is a realistic proverb. Like-minded persons seem to attract and enjoy one another's company, for good or ill. Perhaps even more revealing are the people we dislike or hate. We tend to despise in others what we most fear in ourself.

We find it difficult and challenging to be in the presence of people who seem to have their lives all together and do not need us or our approval at all. They have an inner strength that upsets us. Jesus seems like such a person. The reaction was to kill him.

Prayer. "When the righteous cry for help, the LORD hears" (Psalm 34:17).

Reflection. What about me? Am I defensive when I confront Jesus?

Saturday
of the Fourth Week of Lent

"Why did you not bring him [Jesus] in?" "No man ever spoke like that before," the guards replied. "Do not tell us you too have been taken in!" the Pharisees retorted. (John 7:45–47)

*C*hildren of multinational, multiracial, or multicultural backgrounds come together on a playground and have a great time. Is it possible they are blind to their differences? We adults often make serious decisions about people, countries, customs, or even sports on the flimsiest bits of knowledge or experience. Our parents and our upbringing have often ingrained serious prejudices within our heart. So we rationalize our fear, hatred, segregation, or sexism with arguments that would collapse with the slimmest scrutiny. We get taken in by misinformation.

Jesus, who speaks truth, can often make us defensive. After all, inside we may be more like the Pharisees, who rejected his truth because it upset their narrow worldview. Another part of us knows that we have never heard such welcome words of truth.

Prayer. "God is my shield, / who saves the upright in heart" (Psalm 7:10).

Reflection. Am I open to the words of truth that Jesus is speaking to me this Lent, especially the call to return to him?

Fifth Sunday of Lent (Year A)

Lord, the one you love is sick. *(John 11:3)*

Usually we live our life in Christ as we live the rest of our life in the world. We drift from health to sickness back to health again. Occasional minor indispositions like colds, or major difficulties like a broken bone or pneumonia break into our complacent good health. Eventually we all die of something.

Upon hearing that his friend Lazarus was sick, Jesus said, "This illness does not lead to death; rather it is for God's glory, so that the Son of God may be glorified through it" (John 11:4). God is always Emmanuel, God-with-us. Jesus raised Lazarus from death to manifest God's love and power. Even if we are not cured immediately of a physical illness, God is with us and will bring the type of healing that we most need. Jesus does not sit back and wait for us to come home to his heart, rather he constantly shines the light of his love upon us so that we may find our way back to him.

Prayer. Holy One, I believe that Jesus is the Messiah, the savior of us all.

Reflection. When have I felt Jesus pursuing me? Can I stop running?

Fifth Sunday of Lent (Year B)

"We should like to see Jesus." (John 12:21)

Just like the Greeks in this story who came to the Passover, this should be our dream: "We would like to see Jesus." Ever since God established the covenant with Abraham, the sacred relationship between God and us has been refined. The exterior ordinances and the interior spirit have been steadily aligned. In today's first reading, Yahweh proclaims: "I will be the God of all the families of Israel, and they shall be my people" (Jeremiah 31:1). Saint Paul quotes Jeremiah that Jesus is the mediator of the covenant of love (cf. Hebrews 8:6–12).

Jesus gives us two images that describe following him. One is the grain of wheat that dies to itself in order to become fruitful. The other is those who are detached from life in this world so that they can preserve life in the next: those who die to themselves will see Jesus.

Prayer. "Create in me a clean heart, O God, / and put a new and right spirit within me" (Psalm 51:10).

Reflection. For us the road to glory is power. For Jesus the road to glory is the paschal mystery. What road to glory am I on?

Fifth Sunday of Lent (Year C)

Jesus said, "Nor do I condemn you. You may go. But from now on, avoid this sin." (John 8:11)

The scribes and Pharisees led the woman caught in adultery before Jesus. They made her stand in public shame. They were not interested in her. They sought to trap Jesus into breaking the law of Moses that stated that she should be stoned. The important thing for them was to catch the two lawbreakers, the woman and Jesus. Jesus had been teaching and acting in ways that showed that the Law was made for humans and not humans for the Law.

The priority of love and its power of healing are often attacked by the insecure, who have no love for themselves or others and can maintain control only by rigorous, legalistic interpretations of the norms. Jesus will have none of this kind of legalism. Love comes first.

Prayer. "I want to know Christ and the power of his resurrection and the sharing of his sufferings by becoming like him" (Philippians 3:10).

Reflection. Have I reflected seriously enough on the relationships between justice and love, law and mercy?

Monday
of the Fifth Week of Lent

They suppressed their consciences; they would not allow
their eyes to look to heaven, and did not keep in mind just
judgments. (Daniel 13:9)

From the biblical point of view, every sin is a sin of un-
faithfulness. We do not have to go as far as adultery to be
unfaithful to God or one another as members of the Body of Christ.
The judges in the Susanna story had already committed adultery in
their hearts even though they may not have literally broken a law.
They had suppressed their consciences.

The Pharisees hated Jesus because he insisted on mercy. We
have to look into our own heart over and over again, especially when
we feel we are defending the law and the good of society in emo-
tional and passionate judgments. The only solution is the dictum
of Jesus to not judge unless we are willing to be judged using the
same norms; that is, those who throw stones should not live in glass
houses. The commandments to love are the heavenly law.

Prayer.

Loving God,
even though I walk through the darkest valley,
I fear no evil;
for you are with me.

(Psalm 23:4)

Reflection. Am I free enough to look to heaven and see the
truth as Jesus sees it?

Tuesday
of the Fifth Week of Lent

You belong to this world—
a world which cannot hold me.
(John 8:23)

The essence of God is to be. When Moses asked God what the sacred name was, God replied, "I AM." The creative power of God unleashes all that is, merely by calling it into being. God spoke, and light was made. It is for this reason that we rejoice these days.

By our Baptism, the life of God is in us. Death and the world of selfishness cannot contain us. The "I am" of God is also the love of God. God is love. By sharing "I-am love" with us, God re-creates us over and over again to the sacred likeness and makes us truly human. When we, the Body of Christ, love one another with Christ's love, we also re-create one another to become love, the agape of God. The New Testament's two commandments of love are not legal prescriptions, they are expressions of who God is. They are given to us to enable us to become one with God.

Prayer. God, who is love, lift me up and heal me.

Reflection. Do I believe that by God's gratuitous love the Holy Spirit is within me, that I too am a sacrament of life-giving love?

Wednesday
of the Fifth Week of Lent

If you live according to my teaching,
you are truly my disciples;
then you will know the truth,
and the truth will set you free.
                    (John 8:31)

We continue to feel the spirit of joy as we see more clearly the possibility of breaking the power of sin and death within us. Our hope of growing from inauthenticity to authenticity is real and available. It is the truth that will make us free. If we honestly accept who we are and whose we are and live accordingly, we will be free.

The truth is that we are the children of God, the people of God, the Mystical Body of Christ. Once we admit this, the truth will resonate in our life. This truth will become a brilliant light, enabling us to see ourself in our fullness. This flame of hope will reveal all that we are, all that we are not, and all that we can become.

Prayer. Blessed are you, my God. Make in me a new heart and a new spirit.

Reflection. In practice, what is the basic truth that energizes me and gives me life?

Thursday
of the Fifth Week of Lent

If I glorify myself,
that glory comes to nothing.
(John 8:54)

The intensity of the debate between Jesus and the Pharisees reaches the breaking point. Nothing but death will satisfy his challengers; nothing but complete fidelity to his mission will satisfy Jesus. In today's reading from John, Jesus proclaims himself as "I AM." Moreover, he says that anyone who keeps his word will never see death.

Baptism makes us children of God and heirs of heaven. How can this be? We must believe in Jesus and keep his word. We can pray the word simply by saying, "My Jesus, mercy," the honest, clear, simple admission of our individual sin, our congregation's sin, the sins of the Body of Christ, and the recognition that salvation comes from Christ. Glory comes from Christ, nowhere else.

Prayer. Saving one, you are my God. Remember forever your Covenant. My Jesus, mercy.

Reflection. When I pray for help, do I simply say, "God, I love you and I need you"?

Friday of the Fifth Week of Lent

Put faith in these works,
so as to realize what it means
that the Father is in me
and I in him.

(John 10:38)

To make room in our heart for God's unconditional and all-embracing love is difficult. First we have to believe in such love and then trust in it. We might be tempted to feel that there is no room for maneuvering, for us to be ourselves. We need not trust in abstractions, though. We need only look at Jesus' works: healing, teaching, forgiving, and speaking the Good News to all.

As we approach Holy Week, we must prepare a response to Jesus' invitation to come and follow him. Unlike the Apostles, who knew next to nothing about Jesus when he extended this invitation, we know from the Scriptures and two thousand years of the life of the church that we can put our faith in Jesus' works.

Prayer. Your words, O God, are spirit and life. You have the message of eternal life.

Reflection. What is my response to, "Come follow me"?

Saturday
of the Fifth Week of Lent

Jesus would die for the nation—and not for this nation only, but to gather into one all the dispersed children of God. (John 11:52)

The high priest prophesied that Jesus must die to save the nation, and indeed he did. His blood released the creative power of the Trinity to form the Body of Christ with Jesus as its head and us as its members. A new Israel with a new Covenant was formed, a new testament of love with its law abiding in our heart. This Body of Christ is sacrament to the whole world, making the invisible visible.

The Body of Christ is one as the Trinity is one, each member empowering the other by shared faith, hope, and especially love. The church goes into the world just as Jesus came into the world, that all would be one in him.

Prayer. My Creator, consecrate me in truth, as Jesus was consecrated in truth.

Reflection. Do I see my faith as a gift from God purely for my own benefit or also as an instrument for spreading the Reign of God throughout the world?

Passion Sunday (Palm Sunday)

If they were to keep silence, I tell you the very stones would cry out. (Luke 19:40)

H Holy Week starts out triumphantly. To fulfill the Scriptures, Jesus mounts a donkey, enters Jerusalem, and is received with great acclaim. The public proclamation energizes both Jesus' followers and his enemies.

Palm Sunday is filled with paradox. The people cheering him will later shun him. By killing Jesus, his enemies achieve their victory, but they effectively establish Christ's Reign. By freely becoming obedient unto death, even death on the cross, Jesus receives the name above every other name and releases the creative power of the Trinity to establish God's Reign forever. So the triumphant entry that leads to his horrible death also leads to his triumphant Resurrection.

Prayer. Hosanna! Blessed be he who comes in the name of God.

Reflection. Do I accept the paradoxes of Christian life?

Monday of Holy Week

Here is my servant whom I uphold,
my chosen one with whom I am pleased.
(Isaiah 42:1)

The energy of the Trinity has created the Body of Christ just as it created the human Jesus, the suffering servant. God has chosen us, and we are God's people. As the triune God sent Jesus into the world, so we are sent into the world. Faith is a gift freely given and must be freely accepted. It is of paramount importance that we acknowledge who we are and whose we are. We are the children of God, truly daughters and sons, divinized by our Creator's gratuitous grace. We are the sisters and brothers of Jesus, from whose fullness we have all received. We are the spouse, joy, friend, and love of the Holy Spirit.

This awareness, affirmed in prayer, enables us to live in a special way, the way of Jesus. The church must be the voice of the voiceless poor, binding the bruised reed and fanning the smoldering wick into a fiery flame of love.

Prayer. Gracious God, you are my light and my salvation.

Reflection. Do I deeply acknowledge that I am the spouse, joy, friend, and love of the Holy Spirit?

Tuesday of Holy Week

The Lord called me from birth,
from my Mother's womb he gave me my name.
(Isaiah 49:1)

To be the Body of Christ, the suffering servant, each of us must be aware of our unique gifts. It is much more than cooperation, it is union with God and with one another to be the presence of God's love in the world. Each of us must be humble enough to accept ourself and our responsibility to share ourself with one another and the world.

Another side to humility is also needed to be the Body of Christ. We must be aware of our vulnerability and fragility. A little insecurity goes a long way. Many of us will fall not because we are evil, but because we overestimate our strength and love. Peter exclaimed that he would follow Jesus anywhere, but he denied Jesus three times. Only God's grace makes us truly strong enough to follow our calling.

Prayer. O God, "upon you have I leaned from my birth; / it was you who took me from my mother's womb" (Psalm 71:6).

Reflection. Can I see my unique strengths and weaknesses in my relationship with God and others?

Wednesday of Holy Week

Surely it is not I, Rabbi? (Matthew 26:25)

My name is *mammon* (money). Together with my two cousins, materialism and consumerism, we probably have done more to damage the members of the Body of Christ than sex, drugs, or drink. We are not too subtle. We are more like the air people breathe. We encourage wealth for excellent motives: to contribute to worthy causes, to help the children, and so on. The church itself confers honors on its wealthy contributors. Sometimes clergy work harder at putting up buildings than building the Body of Christ.

Our trick is to ensure that things are preferred over persons. Then children are neglected, the poor are exploited, and wealth becomes security and success. We have a large enrollment in our Iscariot Society. Of all the preaching Jesus did, his blessing on the poor in spirit has to be one of the strongest. There is more or less of Judas Iscariot in all of us: an important consideration for today.

Prayer. "In you, O LORD, I take refuge; / let me never be put to shame" (Psalm 71:1).

Reflection. I must not be of the world any more than Jesus is of the world. True?

Holy Thursday

"If I do not wash you [Peter]," Jesus answered, "you will have no share in my heritage." (John 13:8)

This feast gives us two symbols: the washing of the feet and the celebration of the Eucharist at the Last Supper. Both are signs of one and the same thing: achieving authentic humanity requires self-emptying love. Self-emptying love is the heart of being made in the image and likeness of God. Of the four Gospels, John is the only one that does not record at the Last Supper the words, "This is my body; this is my blood." But in the action of the washing of the feet, what Jesus does not say in words, he says in deed. He gives life to his disciples by telling them that they become themselves by allowing him to love them. Even though they are uncomfortable in the passive position of being loved, it is the only way they can become what they should be.

Jesus then tells the disciples to serve one another and share Communion in memory of him. So as the Body of Christ in, with, and through the heart of Jesus, we offer ourselves in service and communion.

Prayer. Jesus, meek and humble of heart, make my heart like yours.

Reflection. Do I let myself be washed by Jesus so that I can truly be Jesus and wash others?

Good Friday

See, my servant shall prosper,
he shall be raised high and greatly exalted.
(Isaiah 52:11)

G3 Jesus did not choose the cross, he accepted it. As a matter
of fact, Jesus asked that he be spared, but then added, only
if it was his Abba's will:

Being found in human form,
he humbled himself
and became obedient to the point of death—
even death on a cross.

(Philippians 2:8)

Our word *patience* comes from the Latin word *passio,* "to suffer."
Like Jesus, we can accept our cross as it appears in all human life:
the cross of aging, the cross of loss, the cross of the unexpected, the
cross of separation. Accepting these inevitable crosses can help us
to become more human, more loving toward one another.

Another type of cross that helps fashion us to the image and
likeness of God is the cross of fidelity to our faith. Peacefully and
freely living our Christianity daily will stir up opposition and even
hatred because we are not of the world. It is this obedience, listening to the word of Christ, that draws us through the Crucifixion
to the Resurrection.

Prayer. I adore you, O Christ, and I praise you because by
your holy cross, you have redeemed the world.

Reflection. Can I drink the cup that Jesus wishes me to drink?

The Resurrection—Easter

So he [Peter] went away full of amazement at what had occurred. (Luke 24:12)

One Easter Sunday, the entrance hymn "Christ the Lord Is Risen Today, Alleluia" was being sung by the congregation with tremendous enthusiasm. When the final verse was sung, a child shouted out, "Hooray." That was a homily in itself.

Time has a way of dulling our sense of wonder, even about the Resurrection of Jesus. The Resurrection is the most unique of all human experiences. The Holy Spirit of God gave life to a dead man, Jesus. Today is the anniversary of God's victory over sin and death. As sinners now saved, our only fitting response is to burst forth with the Easter Alleluia. We are free to live our new life in Christ. The resurrected life is above all the new life of love.

Prayer. This is the day the Lord has made. Let us rejoice and be glad. Amen! Alleluia!

Reflection. Now, how am I going to live the resurrected life?

Monday of the Octave of Easter

I have set the Lord ever before me,
with him at my right hand
I shall not be disturbed.
　　　(Acts of the Apostles 2:25)

The spirit of God who formed Jesus to be the risen Christ is the same Holy Spirit abiding in our heart. The Spirit is the dynamic agent of life, indwelling in the depth of our heart to form us into God's image, to be truly human. Our life with the Holy Spirit within us is the basis for our Christian humanism. We need not be afraid of the world or anything or anyone. Everything God created is good.

It is when we isolate ourselves from God's presence and saving power that our selfishness takes over and makes us less than we should be. To achieve the ultimate glory of being truly and totally human is impossible for us, but it is not impossible for God, the Holy Spirit.

Prayer. "Come, Holy Spirit, and from heaven direct on [us] the rays of your light. Come, Father of the poor; come, giver of God's gifts; come, light of [our] hearts" (sequence of Pentecost Sunday).

Reflection. What vision do I have of myself? Who do I want to be?

Tuesday of the Octave of Easter

Jesus said to her, "Mary!" She turned to him and said [in Hebrew], "Rabboni!" (meaning "Teacher"). (John 20:16)

When Mary Magdalene saw Jesus at the tomb, she thought he was a gardener. When Jesus called her by name, she heard it in her heart. She recognized Jesus. Nobody said "Mary" like Jesus did. They were soul-friends.

To get below the surface of relationships, a great deal of dying to self must take place. We have to listen with our heart when the Gospel is proclaimed in order to hear the Spirit within us. Christ is calling each of us by name too because Christ wants us to be his soul-friends just like Mary.

Prayer. "O most blessed Light divine, shine within this heart of mine and fill my innermost being" (adapted from sequence of Pentecost Sunday).

Reflection. Do I ever listen to God, myself, or others with depth or reverence?

Wednesday
of the Octave of Easter

He went into the temple with them—walking, jumping about, and praising God. (Acts of the Apostles 3:8)

Were not our hearts burning inside us? (Luke 24:32)

Both of the readings in today's liturgy are filled with great emotion. Neither the cured lame man nor the despondent disciples can contain themselves. After recognizing Jesus, they retrace their steps all the way back to Jerusalem to share the good news of the risen Christ. Their hearts are burning within them. The lame man cannot stop jumping up and down.

Why do we show such little joy and exuberance for our faith, personally and liturgically? Carlo Caretto, the spiritual writer, said: "The pastors in the United States would have a difficult ministry because we have no real need for God." If we truly feel no need for Christ, we might not feel great joy at the Resurrection because we don't feel that we needed saving to begin with.

Prayer. Come, Holy Spirit, fill the hearts of your faithful and enkindle in them the fire of your love. Alleluia.

Reflection. What are the experiences that give me life, that make my heart burn within me? Is Christ one of them?

Thursday of the Octave of Easter

They were still incredulous for sheer joy and wonder. (Luke 24:41)

Many of us have experiences of great joy that at least momentarily we cannot believe. Some of them are short-lived, like scoring a winning goal during the last second of a game. Others are more profound and will demand a lifetime of response because they touch the depth of our being, like falling in love or seeing our child born.

At some point in our life, Jesus has to become that real for us. Then we can accept him or reject him. This should be true for those baptized as infants as well as those who find him later as adult converts. All of us must be converted to Jesus and his lifestyle to be genuine children of God. This is the work of the Spirit. Christians can live a lifetime and not remember who they are.

Prayer. Come, Holy Spirit. Lead that I may see what you have done to me.

Reflection. What is it about Christ that I find wondrous and joyous?

Friday of the Octave of Easter

It is the Lord! (John 21:7)

In this lovely springtime scene, Jesus is watching the Apostles fishing on the Sea of Galilee. After inquiring about their success at fishing that evening, which has been none too good, he tells them to try fishing on the starboard side. They are shocked at the great number of fish they catch. Immediately they experience Jesus' presence. Overjoyed, a naked Peter jumps into the water to get to Christ. Then Christ prepares a fire and they have breakfast together. No question at all, "It is the Lord" (John 21:7). Like the Apostles, we know Christ in the sharing of the sacred meal.

The conviction of Christ's constant presence and power was the Apostles' strength when they began to preach. "By what power or by what name did you do this?" the Sadducees asked at their trial. "By the name of Jesus Christ," Peter replied (Acts of the Apostles 4:7,10).

Prayer. "This is the LORD's doing; / it is marvelous in our eyes" (Psalm 118:23).

Reflection. Do I let God guide and support me on my journey as a born-again person in Christ?

Saturday of the Octave of Easter

Judge for yourselves whether it is right in God's sight for us to obey you rather than God. (Acts of the Apostles 4:19)

The gift of faith is given to us primarily to be shared with others. If those with whom we are sharing are Christians, our living faith should deepen their faith and vice versa. If they are not Christians, our lives should be sacraments of the Holy Spirit's presence to witness to the Spirit's love and power within us.

One of the most challenging experiences for any of us is to encourage people to be true to their word. The most powerful evangelization is to reflect the Word, Jesus, in our daily life. When his values are our values, his dreams our dreams, his message our message, our poverty his riches, power comes forth from us.

Prayer.

Come, Father of the poor!
Come, Source of all our store!
Come, within our bosoms shine!
(Sequence of Pentecost Sunday)

Reflection. "As many of you as were baptized into Christ have clothed yourself with Christ" (Galatians 3:27). Can I say "alleluia" to that?

Second Sunday of Easter (Year A)

Blest are they who have not seen and have believed.
(John 20:29)

None of us has seen the risen Christ, yet generations of Christians have believed. Why does Jesus call us "blessed"? We are blessed because in the mystery of God's love, God has chosen to gift us with faith. Faith is a pure gift. It cannot be earned in any way whatsoever. The miracles of Jesus are not the basis of our faith. We may have a serious illness, and God may or may not heal the illness. If we have faith, we are healed—made whole— nonetheless.

"From his fullness we have all received, grace upon grace. The law indeed was given through Moses; grace and truth came through Jesus Christ. No one has ever seen God. It is God the only Son, who is close to the Father's heart, who has made him known" (John 1:16–18).

Prayer. We give thanks to you, loving God, for the gift of faith. Strengthen it now and lead us to resurrected life.

Reflection. How do I express my gratitude for God's gift of faith?

Second Sunday of Easter (Year B)

Peace be with you. (John 20:19)

Of course the Apostles are afraid when Jesus just appears before them in a locked room. Even after showing his hands and feet, he repeats his greeting of peace. Indeed, so amazing and incredible is the Resurrection that today we still need to be reminded that Jesus wishes us peace. He is the pathway to peace.

The Messiah is to bring peace to people of goodwill (cf. Luke 2:14). Now the Apostles can truly be at peace because Christ has conquered death. The promised Messiah has fulfilled God's promise to Israel. The belief in Jesus and the love that the Apostles offered him were not wasted. Peace has come to them in the presence of the risen Christ. They need never fear again. We need never fear again.

Prayer. "O give thanks to the LORD, for he is good, / for his steadfast love endures forever (Psalm 118:29).

Reflection. I should listen to Christ's words over and over, believing them: Peace be with me.

Second Sunday of Easter (Year C)

Through the hands of the apostles, many signs and wonders occurred among the people. (Acts of the Apostles 5:12)

Jesus had blessed the Apostles with the power to heal, to preach, and to drive out demons, even before his dying and rising. Now after his Resurrection and their empowerment at Pentecost, the Apostles' ministry was marvelous indeed. People would line up on the streets so that Peter's shadow would cross over them and they would be healed.

We might be tempted to forget that we are people of Easter and Pentecost too. The same Spirit that inflamed the Apostles with zeal for Christ, that made them doers of miracles, and that put healing power in their hands is the same Spirit that fills us through Baptism and Confirmation. If we have faith the size of a mustard seed, we can move mountains. We can certainly drive out our personal demons. And so we pray for stronger faith.

Prayer. Come, spirit of the living God, transform my weak faith into the faith of the Apostles.

Reflection. Am I scared of such faith and power, or do I just not believe that this Spirit is in me?

Monday
of the Second Week of Easter

I solemnly assure you,
no one can enter into God's kingdom
without being begotten by water and Spirit.
Flesh begets flesh,
Spirit begets spirit.

(John 3:5–6)

When Jesus began his preaching, his message was exactly the same as that of John the Baptist: "Repent, the Reign of God is at hand." Later on he began to say, "The Reign of God is within you." He taught us this because he is the agent bringing God and us together. The Reign of God is not a place. It is a relationship of shared love between God and us.

Everything else God gives us—the Scriptures, the sacraments, the church—deepens our relationship with God and nourishes the Spirit within us. These relationships draw us to closer relationship with other believers and the whole human family. Spirit begets spirit.

Prayer. "Bless the LORD, O my soul" (Psalm 104:1).

Reflection. How can I become more aware of God's presence within me every moment of the day?

Tuesday
of the Second Week of Easter

The wind blows where it will.

. . . .

So it is with everyone begotten of the Spirit.
(John 3:8)

The Greek word for *wind* means both wind and spirit. The image is used by Jesus to teach us something about the style and power of the Spirit. Surely the Spirit is the God of surprises, blowing where and how the Spirit wills. So in Acts of the Apostles 4:32–37, Barnabas sells his farm and lays all his money at the feet of the Apostles. The entire fledgling community of Jerusalem does the same thing.

The Spirit blows where the Spirit wills, from Francis of Assisi to Dorothy Day, from the First Council of Jerusalem to the fresh air of Vatican Council II. The Spirit blows the life-giving water of Baptism over our sinful self and cleanses us like beautiful seashells on the shore.

Prayer. Come, spirit of God's love, fly me like a kite for your delight.

Reflection. Do I live my life on God's terms or only on my own terms?

Wednesday
of the Second Week of Easter

Yes, God so loved the world
that he gave his only Son,
that whoever believes in him may not die
but may have eternal life.

(John 3:16)

The idea of God being the promised messiah was startling, scandalous, even blasphemous to the most orthodox of the Chosen People. That someone would claim to be Son of God was completely repugnant to them. God was so transcendent that any hint of incarnation, death, and resurrection as an expression of God's love was unthinkable.

The real shock or scandal, though, is that God loves us so much that God became a human, Emmanuel, God-with-us. Even more incredible is the Resurrection that shattered the barrier between life and death. Now there is no death in Christ. If we accept God's saving love, we will never die. Shocking! Marvelous!

Prayer. "O give thanks to the LORD, for he is good; / his steadfast love endures forever!" (Psalm 118:1).

Reflection. The realization and constant awareness of God's love for me is far more important than my desire to love God. Can I believe that?

Thursday
of the Second Week of Easter

Better for us to obey God than men! (Acts of the Apostles 5:29)

Humans measure out their love in teaspoons for some, ladles for others, and eyedroppers for still others. God's love is far more profligate. God just loves unconditionally, totally, passionately. Better that we obey this God of love than people who would warn us away from such Godlike love.

Jesus called us to witness to God's love flowing through our daily experience of family life, work, hopes, and desires. To compartmentalize our faith, love, and hope is to obey humans rather than God. The God of Sunday is also the God of Thursday. God does not ration the Spirit.

Prayer. Loving God, help me to love and not count the cost.

Reflection. What would Jesus accept and what would he reject of the so-called American Dream?

Friday
of the Second Week of Easter

A vast crowd kept following him because they saw the signs he was performing for the sick. (John 6:1)

All of us have deep hungers in our heart. We have a hunger for a better marriage, for our children to find peace, for an end to our loneliness, for our love for Jesus to deepen.

Jesus is the divine healer, but in the Gospels he does not heal everyone physically. He uses their immediate hunger to lead them more deeply into a healing relationship with God, with their neighbors, and within themselves. Jesus feeds their hunger, but when they wish to crown him king, he will have none of it. The Reign of God in which all have what they need and all live with God transcends time and place.

Prayer. Our Father, thy kingdom come.

Reflection. Why do I follow Jesus? What do I expect of him?

Saturday
of the Second Week of Easter

It is not right for us to neglect the word of God in order to wait on tables. (Acts of the Apostles 6:2)

The church is the Body of Christ. It has an obligation to be catholic, that is, universal. It should be open to all cultures, all persons—male and female, all classes—rich and poor, all gifts—great and small. The church's history is marred by various persons and groups excluding or dominating others because of fear and insecurity. The church has often wounded itself more than its enemies have.

We have neglected the Word to build buildings and not community. We have divided into factions, each claiming to be more Christian than the other. Narrow theological hairsplitting has replaced openness to the word of God. But the resurrected life that Christ offers never neglects the word of God because only it can bring fullness of life.

Prayer. Your words, O Christ, are spirit and truth. May we never neglect them.

Reflection. Do I neglect the Word while "waiting on tables"?

Third Sunday of Easter (Year A)

Were not our hearts burning inside us as he talked to us on the road and explained the Scriptures to us! (Luke 24:32)

Today's liturgy teaches us about the relationship between God's word and seeing Jesus with our heart. Jesus shares a simple, ordinary meal with the brokenhearted and despairing disciples on the way to Emmaus. They had staked everything on the conviction that Jesus was the Messiah. Now he was dead and gone. It was all over. Then Jesus joins them, shares his word and the Hebrew Scriptures with them, and something is stirred in their hearts. No one had ever talked to them like the risen Christ did. They recognize him as he breaks and shares the bread.

If we open ourself to Christ's word and the Spirit within us, reading with our heart as well as our eyes, Jesus will reveal himself in many diverse experiences. The presence of Jesus in his word and the hunger in our heart will become a shining light in the darkness.

Prayer. Risen Christ, make my heart burn with love for you.

Reflection. How can I invite the fire of Christ's love into my heart?

Third Sunday of Easter (Year B)

You are witnesses of this. (Luke 24:48)

The disciples who experienced the risen Christ on the way to Emmaus retrace their steps to share their experience with the others. As they are speaking, Jesus himself appears. The disciples think that they are seeing a ghost. To help them, Jesus asks them to touch him. He also asks for food, and once again explains his life and words as the fulfillment of the Law of Moses. The scene ends with Jesus telling them that they must be witnesses to his life.

Words are not enough to witness to resurrection. The Resurrection invites us to live a new life in Christ. The world of nonbelievers has a right to "touch" us and see if we are real. If our church does not live and preach Jesus as crucified and risen, no one has the need to follow. If the church does not proclaim Jesus in our ordinary experience, we have nothing distinctive to offer.

Prayer. "Let the light of your face shine on us, / O LORD" (Psalm 4:6).

Reflection. Are my actions speaking as loudly or more loudly than my words? What are they saying?

Third Sunday of Easter (Year C)

Peter said to them, "I'm going out to fish." (John 21:3)

After the Resurrection, Christ appears twice to his Apostles. The Resurrection does not seem to have turned their lives around much. Peter tells the others that he is going fishing. They join him. He is not fishing for people. He is going back to his old job as if nothing had happened.

Finally, Jesus appears on the scene. It is reminiscent of the early days when he first sought them out and called them to follow him. It is heartwarming that Jesus keeps seeking us out. It is frightening that we so easily forget or cannot integrate our faith into our daily life. Our churches are jam-packed on Easter, but much less so the following Sunday. Never fear, Jesus is always fishing for us anyway.

Prayer.

Heal our wounds, our strength renew;
On our dryness pour your dew;
Wash the strains of guilt away.
(Sequence of Pentecost Sunday)

Reflection. Only in the power of the Spirit can we keep ourselves alive. So how alive am I?

Monday
of the Third Week of Easter

You should not be working for perishable food.
(John 6:27)

The great Resurrection gift of Jesus to us is the Holy Spirit bestowed on us in Baptism. To genuinely accept the presence of the Spirit on our life journey is the basic "work" of the Christian, personally and as a church. Sometimes we think of ourself as called to practice faith and good works. Actually, *the* good work is to cultivate our faith, the activity of God's spirit within us. The Spirit shapes us to be God's glory. Good works follow.

If we think that we have to work our way to God through various devotions, religious gatherings, or good deeds, we may be simply following our will, not that of the Spirit. We can be so full of our own spiritual activity that we are like moving targets—even the Holy Spirit cannot hit us. On the other hand, if we listen carefully to the growing seed of the Spirit within us, it blossoms into hope and love.

Prayer. "Come, Holy Spirit. Soften the hard heart, we are the ice-cold heart. Give direction to the wayward heart" (adapted from sequence of Pentecost Sunday).

Reflection. God's gift of the Spirit adds a new dimension to my life. Have I accepted the gift?

Tuesday
of the Third Week of Easter

I myself am the bread of life.
(John 6:35)

Actually believing that Jesus is the bread of life challenges the faith of Christians. According to polls and the anecdotal evidence of pastors and parish ministers, a large percentage of Catholics do not affirm the real presence of Christ in the Eucharist. How contradictory is it, though, that the vast majority of parents are adamant concerning their children "making" first (and perhaps last) Communion.

Jesus declares that he is the bread of life. Can a Christian really turn down the bread of life and expect to live the resurrected life of Christ? Hardly.

Prayer. Come, Bread of Life and Cup of Blessing. Feed me and nourish me to resurrected life.

Reflection. Do I truly believe Jesus is the bread of life?

Wednesday
of the Third Week of Easter

It is the will of him who sent me
that I should lose nothing of what he has given me.
(John 6:39)

Jesus went from death to life. Receiving the Bread of Life takes us from death to eternal life. In the breaking of the bread and sharing of the cup, the early Christians experienced joy.

They were beaten and martyred for preaching the Gospel, but their hearts were filled with joy because they shared Christ's suffering, as he had suffered for them. It was a joy that triumphed over the daily trials of life. It was a joy that sustained them, coming from a genuine communion with the one they loved, the risen Christ. This Resurrection faith made them alive and joyful. "Alleluia" is the true song of all Christians.

Prayer. Alleluia! "Make a joyful noise to God, all the earth" (Psalm 66:1).

Reflection. Do I truly believe that "the Spirit helps us in our weakness"? (Romans 8:26).

Thursday
of the Third Week of Easter

"They shall all be taught by God."
Everyone who has heard the Father
and learned from him
comes to me.

(John 6:45)

The gift of faith is exactly that, a pure gift. God knows why the gift has been given to us. Our responsibility is just to accept the gift. What does that entail? First and above all, it means appreciating the gift. This is done by letting the Gift Giver speak to us. We must take time to pray, to reflect together with God and others about the mystery of God's giving.

Do not be afraid: we will usually feel tugs between belief and unbelief. Voicing our inner struggles will be a blessing. The Spirit is ever present in our heart and where two or three gather to find truth. God is always teaching. We need only to be listening.

Prayer. God, I am not worthy, but say the word and my spirit will be healed.

Reflection. When it comes to being taught by God, am I sitting in the front of class ready to take notes, or am I sitting in back half-asleep?

Friday
of the Third Week of Easter

The man who feeds on my flesh
and drinks my blood
remains in me, and I in him.
(John 6:56)

Jesus bluntly tells us that either we let him share his divinity with us or we have no life. The eucharistic presence of Jesus is the source of our life. It is not a quantitative or mere biological presence. It is the food of our born-again life, making us into his image and likeness. This divine food makes us divine.

The "amen" of eucharistic reception is the sign for this covenant of love demanded by God for this gift of Jesus. We live in him. The suffering, death to self, and resurrection that come from our shared life is the stuff of our growth. When we digest our natural food, we become human. When we digest the Eucharist, we share in divinity.

Prayer. Jesus, meek and humble of heart, make my heart like unto yours.

Reflection. Have I been fed by the Bread of Life?

Saturday
of the Third Week of Easter

Many of the disciples of Jesus remarked, "This sort of talk is hard to endure! How can anyone take it seriously?" (John 6:60)

It is easy to have sympathy for Christians and non-Christians who heard Jesus talking about being the bread of life and about his words being spirit and truth. It was startling. Peter has the only answer possible: "Lord, to whom can we go? You have the words of eternal life" (John 6:68).

Faith is a pure gift. Nothing challenges us more than accepting and living this gift. We are the same persons and yet very different owing to our Baptism. We must live in the world the same as others, and yet we no longer live because Christ lives in us. "This sort of talk is hard to endure" unless we embrace God's grace to believe.

Prayer. "Jesus, Lord of the impossible, have mercy on us" (Charles de Foucauld).

Reflection. Can I endure listening to and believing in the words of eternal life?

Fourth Sunday of Easter (Year A)

I am the sheepgate.
. . . .
*Whoever enters through me
will be safe.*

(John 10:9)

During his lifetime, Jesus told us that as they persecuted him, so they will persecute us. Both the Acts of the Apostles and the Book of Revelation record how it started immediately. Paul and Barnabas are expelled from a town for preaching fearlessly (cf. Acts of the Apostles, chapters 13–14). Revelation speaks of the ones "who have come out of the great ordeal" (7:14).

The risen Christ continues to love us and will always protect us and be present to us. Jesus assures us that no one will snatch us away. As Isaiah promised, God will keep us in the palm of the sacred hands. We must make every effort to listen for the voice of the Spirit to genuinely follow our Shepherd. The conviction of Christ's presence and protection should remove the fear that so often paralyzes our response.

Prayer.

The LORD is God.
It is he that made us, and we are his;
we are his people, and the sheep of his pasture.

(Psalm 100:3)

Reflection. Does fear diminish my total response to the Gospel?

Fourth Sunday of Easter (Year B)

The Father loves me for this:
that I lay down my life.
(John 10:13)

Jesus and the Father have a unique relationship. Jesus is the Son of God. As such, he was obedient to the Father. He emptied himself and became obedient to death, even death on a cross (cf. Philippians 2:7–8). Jesus knew the difficulties and trials that went with his mission. Out of love for the Father and us, he gave himself to the work of redemption for us all.

What Jesus did was done out of love. Now Baptism gives us a new life in Christ, letting us be called the children of God. That is what we are (cf. 1 John 3:1). As God's children, we are given the grace to "lay down" our life for the good of God's people, usually by small sacrifices—getting up in the middle of the night to nurse an infant, visiting a lonely, elderly uncle in a nursing home, and so on. Thus we become Jesus' sisters and brothers, his family.

Prayer. Father, your will be done.

Reflection. God has given me the same Spirit given to Jesus. How is this Spirit leading me to "lay down" my life?

Fourth Sunday of Easter (Year C)

No one shall snatch them out of my hand.
(John 10:28)

This is one of the most comforting passages of the New Testament. Jesus promises us that no one will steal us from him. Not only that, but no one will snatch us from the embrace of God. Jesus gives us assurance that all will be well. The journey of life will be difficult, but it will be successful by God's power and presence.

The condition for the protection and safety is that we obey. The word *obey* comes from *obedire,* to listen. Like the sheep listening to their protecting shepherd, we must listen for the will of God. We must not follow any other voice, no matter how attractive it may sound. The sound of music is not always our song. The word of God must be paramount.

Prayer. "Your statutes have been my songs / wherever I make my home" (Psalm 119:54).

Reflection. How do I as a Christian discern the will of God on a day-to-day basis?

Monday
of the Fourth Week of Easter

I came
that they might have life
and have it to the full.
(John 10:10)

Jesus uses the image of a gate to describe himself as one
who accomplishes the twofold purpose of a gate: to keep
evil out and let good in. This image is not only a symbol of Jesus
but also of the church, each of us individually and as a community.

In her testament to her sisters, Clare of Assisi used the symbol
of a mirror to express the same notion. She told the sisters that
Jesus mirrored God for Francis. Francis mirrored Christ for Clare.
Clare mirrored Jesus for her sisters, and they were to mirror Christ
for one another and for all who encountered them in and out of the
convent. Each of us personally should mirror Jesus. Our family, our
congregation, and the universal church should reflect the power of
the Spirit within us. Life in the Spirit is a full life indeed.

Prayer. Send forth your light and your fidelity, O spirit of God,
and they shall lead me on.

Reflection. What life-giving image do I project?

Tuesday
of the Fourth Week of Easter

My sheep hear my voice.
I know them,
and they follow me.
> *(John 10:27)*

The people ask Jesus not to keep them in suspense. He replies, "I have told you, and you do not believe" (John 10:25). People have many reasons for not believing or acting on the promptings of the Holy Spirit. Fear of losing family, friends, comfort, position, and social standing are always powerfully present. What should we do to give assent to God? With as much sincerity as possible, we should admit our doubts and fears and ask the Holy Spirit to help us follow Jesus.

Though Jesus may call us to let go of bad habits, possessions that possess us, and other things, no one will snatch him out of our hands. Following Jesus is not just a matter of firm resolutions and determination, we must wholeheartedly invite the presence of the Spirit into our life.

Prayer.

Where you are not, man has naught,
nothing good in deed or thought,
> Nothing free from taint of ill.
> (Sequence of Pentecost Sunday)

Reflection. Nothing is impossible for God. Right?

Wednesday
of the Fourth Week of Easter

They imposed hands on them and sent them off . . . by the Holy Spirit. (Acts of the Apostles 13:3–4)

The final step on our journey is to see God face to face. It is hoped that by then we will have truly and even perhaps completely become "other Christs," images of God. However, before we reach the end, we set off on other journeys in life. We pursue all sorts of vocations, avocations, and relationships. In all these many pursuits, we have within us the holy spirit of God gently but firmly assisting us in living Jesus' way.

The consolation of the Spirit's power and presence is a great joy. No matter how old or how young we are, being aware that the Spirit is with us every minute is a tremendous source of hope and patience, enabling us to carry on. The Spirit is God's gift and promise that we will not be left in the dark.

Prayer. May God have pity on us and bless us. May God's face shine upon us.

Reflection. Awareness of the Spirit should draw me to make choices between light and darkness on my journey. Am I following my headlight?

Thursday
of the Fourth Week of Easter

I solemnly assure you,
no slave is greater than his master;
no messenger outranks the one who sent him.
(John 13:16)

During the last half of the Easter season, we pray chapters 13 to 20 of John's Gospel. At the heart of these chapters is this message: "If you know these things, you are blessed if you do them" (John 13:17). Jesus tells us that he knows those he has chosen, those upon whom he has conferred his spirit to be church.

We will not always be readily accepted because he was not readily accepted. Nor will we always be faithful as he was always faithful. It is our awareness of the power and presence of the Spirit both in our moments of fidelity and infidelity that will sustain us to continue the struggle to follow Jesus' journey.

Prayer.

In our labor, rest most sweet;
Grateful coolness in the heat;
> Solace in the midst of woe.
(Sequence of Pentecost Sunday)

Reflection. "My grace is sufficient for you, for power is made perfect in weakness" (2 Corinthians 12:9). What power do I need perfected in my weakness?

Friday
of the Fourth Week of Easter

I am the way, and the truth, and the life.
(John 14:6)

In today's Gospel, Jesus gives himself three titles that might be accepted as a mini-outline of his work. Jesus is "the way" in a twofold sense: first, he is the one who made salvation possible by his Passion, death, Resurrection, and sending forth of his spirit to be our companion. We must have absolute allegiance to him as the center of our life. Second, we must live his way. In fact, the early Christians were called members of the Way: "Let the same mind be in you that was in Christ" (Philippians 2:5).

He is "the truth." Our choices should be based on the will of God as exemplified in the life of Jesus. By the power of the Spirit within us, we come to know the truth and the will of God. Jesus is "the life" because he shares himself with us. If we live his way in truth, we will be one with him, the source of life.

Prayer. O God, send forth your love and your fidelity, and the Spirit shall lead me on.

Reflection. "How can we know the way?" (John 14:5). Have I read the Scriptures or simply called on the Spirit lately?

Saturday
of the Fourth Week of Easter

The man who has faith in me
will do the works I do,
and greater far than these.
            (John 14:12)

We are constantly confronted with the humility of Jesus. His love knows no bounds, but he assures us that his grace will lead us to greater deeds. How is that possible?

It is possible because he has freed us to say "Amen, Alleluia" in his name. Jesus has freed us to be sacraments in the hands of his creative spirit dwelling in us and in the church. As Christians, we have to be humble and grateful to God for the gift of the Spirit, who makes us life-giving agents to the world.

Prayer. Holy One, keep us attentive to the life around us, ready to embrace the Gospels and put your word into action.

Reflection. What deeds of goodness have I done, and what deeds is the grace of God calling me to do?

Sunday of the Fifth Week of Easter (Year A)

I am the way, and the truth, and the life.
(John 14:6)

When Jesus declared that he was "the way, and the truth, and the life," he must have startled Thomas, who had asked, "How can we know the way?" (John14:5). Indeed, the idea of "the way" was dear to the Jewish people. Moses told them, "Follow exactly the path that the Lord your God has commanded you" (Deuteronomy 5:33). Isaiah spoke of the way people would find God's road (cf. Isaiah 30:21). Now Jesus is saying, "I am the way." It is not a set of directions. He is saying, "I am with you; I will accompany you, guide you, and protect you."

How do we accept him as our way? The answer is given in the church: "But you are a chosen race, a royal priesthood, a holy nation, God's own people, in order that you may proclaim the mighty acts of him who called you out of darkness into his marvelous light" (1 Peter 2:9). The church is God's gift to us to point us toward Jesus and to continue his saving work.

Prayer. "Teach me your way, O LORD" (Psalm 27:11).

Reflection. Do I point the way for myself and for others to Jesus, the way?

Sunday of the Fifth Week of Easter (Year B)

*My Father has been glorified
in your bearing much fruit.*
(John15:8)

Every generation of believers from the earliest days has had to reflect on its culture in order to grow and bear fruit. One church document after another has reminded us that we must move beyond private morality to communal morality. We are the people of God, a global village, all of us inextricably linked together. So we are called to be responsible for the whole human family and to reap a harvest of justice.

Even so, our children play with toys made by children in poor countries who are abused and underpaid. The same can be said of designer jeans, running shoes, and so on. Jesus' values are ignored, and much of our daily life can veer toward a kind of paganism in its excesses. The children of God will not bear fruit until the church turns toward deeds of justice and away from greed, consumerism, and exploitation.

Prayer. "Let us love, not in word or speech, but in truth and action" (1 John 3:18).

Reflection. Have I gradually and imperceptibly reconciled myself to injustice?

Sunday of the Fifth Week of Easter (Year C)

Such as my love has been for you,
so must your love be for each other.
(John 13:34)

At Easter, Christ elevates all life by the power of the Resurrection. A new birth has come; a new level of creation is conceived: "See, I am making all things new" (Revelation 21:5). The waters of Baptism have initiated a new lifestyle in Christ.

We can live and grow into true maturity because grace enables us to live the life of divine love. God is love, and for us to be truly alive, we must live God's love. This is possible only by dying to self and invoking the Spirit. We then become the new creation, filled with abundant life.

Prayer. Christ, our life, helps us to live our new life of love.

Reflection. How do I love? Whom do I love?

Monday
of the Fifth Week of Easter

The Paraclete, the Holy Spirit,
whom the Father will send in my name,
will instruct you in everything,
and remind you of all that I told you.
(John 14:26)

Jesus is not speaking simply of knowledge from the mind but of understanding and wisdom from the heart. If we open our heart, mind, and will to the Holy Spirit, we will be taught "everything" that is true, good, and beautiful.

Such wisdom of the Spirit can be as instant as e-mail, but usually comes piece by piece as we learn from each experience. The gifts of the Spirit increase our power for good. In fact, the Paraclete is the only one who can instruct the people of the new creation. But the Spirit speaks to us in the quiet of prayer, in the lonely, hungry heart.

Prayer.

Come, Holy Spirit, come!
And from your celestial home
    Shed a ray of light divine!
(Sequence of Pentecost Sunday)

Reflection. To pray is to give in to truth. Have I surrendered yet?

Tuesday
of the Fifth Week of Easter

My peace is my gift to you.
(John 14:27)

Christians often forget that the last words of Christ were not those spoken from the cross but those spoken after Christ rose from the tomb. His words indicate what the resurrected life was to be: "Peace." Each time he appears to the terrified Apostles, Christ greets them with "Peace," like saying, "It's okay. I am here."

Dante hints at the nature of Christ's wish: "In his will is our peace." If we try to live the Gospel values and use them to prioritize our decisions and hopes, we will experience God's presence and comfort. If we live in the Spirit, times of trial and trouble can also be met peacefully. Only the Spirit can give peace in difficulty because through the Spirit, Jesus conquered the world.

Prayer. To you, O God, I lift up my soul. Grant me your peace.

Reflection. Aren't loving God and loving my neighbor the only ways I will ever find the peace that Christ wants for me?

Wednesday
of the Fifth Week of Easter

I am the vine, you are the branches.
(John 15:5)

The image of the vine and the branches is Jesus' image of the church. Several basic truths are expressed by this metaphor. First of all, Jesus is the vine. All true life is in Christ and flows from him. Second, the branches—the people of God—must be united with him in a genuine union of vision, love, and acceptance of his will.

Third, for us to be life-giving branches, we need pruning over and over again of the grime and fungi that infect us with weakness and fragility. Resurrected life is always about dying and rising, letting go and receiving.

Prayer. Jesus, help me to seek the things of life, not death.

Reflection. What pruning have I gone through, and what still needs to be pruned?

Thursday
of the Fifth Week of Easter

Live on in my love.
(John 15:10)

Through Baptism we have become God's children. This can never be undone. We can be forgetful, unappreciative, irresponsible, or ungrateful, but the fact remains that we are God's children. We live on in God's love. Jesus tells us that this will happen if we keep his Commandments. And even when we break the Commandments, God does not withdraw love, we withdraw from love.

We do not create the union with God. It is there. Prayer is an attempt to help us realize the beauty and truth of what already exists. We are one with God, and God's joy in our love becomes our joy in God's love.

Prayer. "Rejoice in the Lord always; again I will say, Rejoice" (Philippians 4:4).

Reflection. The Kingdom of God is within me!

Friday
of the Fifth Week of Easter

I call you friends.
(John 15:15)

This declaration expresses again the fullness of the Incarnation. Christ calls us friends. By sending his Spirit into our heart, he makes us his friends. Believers of other faiths find such a notion to be outrageously bold. God's friends indeed! Friendship implies a community and a certain equality. Christ calls us friends because he has shared with us the mystery of divine love.

Friendship is based on sharing our life, our dreams, our values, our goods. Too often, though, we have been neither humble enough nor bold enough to make the divine friendship the basis of our daily life. We have taken the road of cheap grace—adhering to laws and rituals—and have shunned the costly grace of love's commitment.

Prayer. Christ, my friend. My friend, Christ.

Reflection. Do I ever feel or speak of Jesus with the ease and comfort that I enjoy with other friends?

Saturday
of the Fifth Week of Easter

If you belonged to the world,
it would love you as its own.
(John 15:19)

Today's world presents a great challenge to the believer. Jesus tells us that we cannot have God and *mammon.* Many of us try to have both. This is a subtle, diabolical temptation. We are tempted to substitute wealth, power, being on the right side, and never breaking ranks with social norms for the Good News, "the way, the truth, and the life" of Christ.

Mammon moves Jesus to the periphery of life and focuses our attention on things that will rust and fade. Our souls are in peril if we belong to the world and are embraced too warmly by its values.

Prayer. Gracious God, light to the world, that I may see.

Reflection. Those who hear the word of God and keep it are Christ's sisters and brothers. Well, am I one of the family?

Sixth Sunday of Easter (Year A)

[God] will give you another Paraclete—
to be with you always.

.   .   .   .

I will not leave you orphaned.
(John 14:16–18)

Jesus is leaving, but he will not leave us unaided in our call. He will send the Holy Spirit, who will be with us day in and day out. The Spirit will dwell within us, so that we can never be orphaned. The Paraclete helps us persevere in our call to be children of God.

Jesus calls the Paraclete the spirit of Truth. This Truth is not a set of doctrines or moral teachings. The Truth is more than that; it is total Truth gained only in an intimate relationship of love in which each of the beloveds knows through love the mind, heart, and will of the other. Knowing Christ, we know the whole Truth that will never leave us alone, afraid, unprotected, and unloved.

Prayer. God, our light, source of all our gifts, send us your spirit.

Reflection. I am not alone. I am not left an orphan. How does this make me feel?

Sixth Sunday of Easter (Year B)

It was not you who chose me,
it was I who chose you
to go forth and bear fruit.
(John 15:16)

"I chose you." When we look back over our life, it is easy to recall the joy when someone chose us. We might have been chosen to accompany our parents someplace special. We might have been chosen to be in a school play. Being chosen gives us great joy and makes us happy and pleased that we are who we are.

Jesus' choosing us should evoke the same response. The joy is even heightened when we realize what we have been chosen for: to live in his love, to become partners and friends rather than servants and slaves, to become fruitful.

Prayer. I rejoice, my God, in being chosen. All praise and thanks to you, Holy Friend.

Reflection. How do I feel to be chosen to dance with God, to be on God's team? What dance will we dance? What position will I play?

Sixth Sunday of Easter (Year C)

I saw no temple in the city. The Lord, God the Almighty, is its temple—he and the Lamb. (Revelation 21:22)

A few years ago, an arsonist set an Episcopal church on fire. I hurried over to see if I could be of help. When I saw the pastor, we embraced. He had tears in his eyes as he said, "They burned down our church." Trying to cheer him, I looked him in the eye and said, "Jerry, they burned the *building*, your beautiful *church* will build you a new one." He smiled and said, "That's great. Thank you."

It is important for us to realize that we are the Body of Christ. We are the church. By the power of the Spirit, we are one people, each with his or her uniqueness. As a strong community, we witness to the Gospel by our fidelity to the Word and God's words.

Prayer. Come, Holy Spirit. We, the faithful, adore and confess you evermore.

Reflection. What part do I play in the Body of Christ?

Monday
of the Sixth Week of Easter

The Spirit of truth . . .

will bear witness on my behalf.
You must bear witness as well.
(John 15:26–27)

Through Baptism, we are no longer the same. We are new creatures in Christ, sharing the divine life of the Trinity. The Spirit of life has restored us to our original beauty, making us worthy disciples of Jesus. As sharers in the divine glory, children of God, and heirs of heaven, we bear a likeness to Jesus, our brother, destined to spread the Reign of God now and forever.

This is the truth, the bottom line of who we are. To live any life other than the life of the Spirit is to be an impostor, to live a lie. "If we say that we have fellowship with [God] while we are walking in darkness, we lie and do not do what is true" (1 John 1:6).

Prayer. Spirit of truth, I believe, help my unbelief.

Reflection. How hard is it to accept the depth of intimacy to which God calls me?

Tuesday
of the Sixth Week of Easter

If I go,
I will send [the Paraclete] to you.
                    (John 16:7)

Jesus had to ascend for the Spirit to come because God wished to reach the minds and hearts of all people, in all places, in all time. The risen Christ appeared in a particular time and place. The Spirit is always present, acting, inspiring, drawing us to resurrected life.

Nevertheless, Jesus kept assuring his disciples that they would not be alone, that he would be with them in the Spirit. This Spirit would lead them to call for repentance, to heal the suffering, to preach the Good News. These are the works of the Spirit. They are not the results of theology but of faith given by the Spirit.

Prayer. "I give you thanks, O LORD, with my whole heart" (Psalm 138:1).

Reflection. In a culture of exceptional achievers, can I accept my helplessness and dependence on the Spirit of truth?

Wednesday
of the Sixth Week of Easter

[The Spirit] will guide you to all truth.
(John 16:13)

The presence of the Spirit will guide us in our ways, as a community and as individuals. The community has taken diverse positions that in hindsight do not look too Christian: for example, the Crusades and the Inquisition. But the Spirit has always brought forth leaders and communities to call the church to reform and repentance: for example, Francis of Assisi and Teresa of Ávila, John XXIII and Mother Teresa, Vatican Council II and the Catholic Worker Movement.

As individuals, we make Faustian bargains with consumerism and politics. But the Spirit still enlightens us to random acts of kindness, tender care of our children, courage in defending helpless coworkers, and so on. In short, the Spirit does guide us—always and powerfully.

Prayer. Come, Holy Spirit, help us with renewed energy to continue the saving work begun at Baptism.

Reflection. Have my community and I started the renewal of the church called for in Vatican Council II?

Ascension Thursday

God mounts his throne to shouts of joy.
(Psalm 47:6)

Today we celebrate Christ's Ascension into heaven to be acclaimed as the conqueror of sin and death. Luke says that the disciples returned "to Jerusalem with great joy" (24:52), and they began immediately to spread the Good News, even in the Temple.

Before Christ ascended, he commissioned his followers to "make disciples of all nations" (Matthew 28:19). To withstand the trials that would face them in doing so, Christ reassured them, "I am with you always" (28:20). These words are spoken to us today. Christ's spirit gives joy; now we can go forth.

Prayer. Christ has risen and ascended. Praise to you, our Savior, on this sacred day of victory.

Reflection. Am I ready to make disciples of all nations? Have I made a disciple of myself?

Friday
of the Sixth Week of Easter

You will grieve for a time,
but your grief will be turned into joy.
(John 16:20)

Even though the resurrected Christ ascended to glory, and the disciples left rejoicing, they remembered his admonition to "take up your cross and follow me." The cross and the Resurrection are both part of the deal. Only by accepting both realities can we be thoroughly unified with Jesus. We have to make choices.

As Jesus explains, a woman giving birth experiences great pain, but the joy of having the child pushes the pain into the background. So also if we lead a truly Christian life we will have the joy of union with Jesus, but first we may suffer for our friendship with Christ.

Prayer. Christ, may I always rest in the reassurance of your promises.

Reflection. What crosses am I carrying right now? What sort of help do I need to carry them?

Saturday
of the Sixth Week of Easter

Ask and you shall receive,
that your joy may be full.
(John 16:24)

In this passage, Jesus is about to die and thus speaks plainly. He is the one whom the Jewish people have been waiting for. Now he will return to heaven. If they believe in him, they are free to go to God directly, asking for whatever graces they need so that their joy will be complete.

In effect, Jesus reminds them that his mission was to tell us that God is love. He was sent because God loved the world. After the death and Resurrection of Jesus, we are free to speak for ourself, petition God for ourself. If we accept Jesus, we are one with him, and through him we are one with God.

Prayer. You said for me to ask, and so I do. Holy One, this is what I need [mention your needs].

Reflection. As time goes on, relationships normally change and grow. Is my relationship with God more mature today than it was before?

Seventh Sunday of Easter (Year A)

It is in them that I have been glorified.
I am in the world no more,
but these are in the world
as I come to you.

(John 17:10–11)

On this Sunday between Ascension and Pentecost, the Apostles were told to wait for the Spirit before they went out to teach all nations. It was necessary to wait for two reasons: first, to appreciate what Jesus had given them, and second, to have the courage to live a new life in Christ.

Christ had come to infuse humanity with new life, the living life of the Trinity. His whole life was a gradual elevating of us to a new level. By his Passion, death, and Resurrection, Jesus witnessed to God's love for us. It is now up to us to glorify God as Christ glorified us. We must live the resurrected life of fidelity to God's word. The church is filled with all sorts of programs for evangelization, but the only effective evangelization comes when we personally and communally live the life of the crucified Christ.

Prayer. O God, let me see all "as rubbish, in order that I may gain Christ" (Philippians 3:8).

Reflection. What would be telltale signs in my life and the life of my community that we have accepted Christ?

Seventh Sunday of Easter (Year B)

Consecrate them by means of truth—
"Your word is truth."

(John 17:17)

Christians have been set apart, consecrated in truth as Jesus was set apart. The truth, the word, is that we are the children of God. We are forever marked by that sign at Baptism. We are in the world, but we must not be of the world. We must remember who we are and Whose we are. We belong to God and to one another. Our lives must be characterized by love because "God is love, and those who abide in love abide in God, and God abides in them" (1 John 4:16).

The road we have to travel is narrow, and the city we wish to enter has a narrow gate for entrance. Only by living for and in Christ can we complete the journey successfully. We do not have to fear sin as long as we are striving to follow Christ. His mercy will use our weaknesses for a greater love. We have to fear indifference perhaps most of all.

Prayer. Spirit of the living God, let nothing ever come between us (cf. Romans 8:38–39).

Reflection. What does it mean for me to be anointed and consecrated to the risen Savior?

Seventh Sunday of Easter (Year C)

I do not pray for my disciples alone.
I pray also for those who will believe in me . . .
that all may be one.

(John 17:20–21)

Jesus' prayer is twofold. He prays for those who would believe in him through the word of the disciples, and he prays that through this unity of believers the world would believe that Jesus is the one sent to save us.

The unity Jesus is referring to is not a unity of administration or organization. It is not even an ecclesiastical unity. It is a personal unity of sisters and brothers who accept Jesus as redeemer. It is a unity of human beings who accept one another with respect and appreciation. In a family, each child has her or his own gifts. If family members love and respect one another, they become a family. Just so, Christian unity should transcend differences because it is of the Spirit.

Prayer. May we be one, O God, as you and Jesus are one.

Reflection. What am I willing to do to promote the cause of Christian unity?

Monday
of the Seventh Week of Easter

We do indeed believe you came from God. (John 16:30)

In this passage, we see a change in the Apostles. They finally understand Jesus, but he makes the point that understanding is not enough. Without the Spirit's presence, they will scatter and go their own way. He tells them this so that they will not be destroyed by their own weakness and fear. Jesus, the thoughtful friend, anticipates their sorrow and seeks to alleviate their fear.

Saying that we believe and living in that belief are not quite the same things. We have to live the message of Jesus to be his disciples. Then Jesus' compassion and understanding will be our peace. We will suffer, but we will conquer the world in Christ. His victory will be our victory by the gifts that the Spirit will confer on us.

Prayer. To you, O God, belong all glory, praise, and thanks.

Reflection. God's ways are surely not my ways. Weak as I am, I have been chosen to spread the Good News (cf. 1 Corinthians 1:27–31). Where and how do I start, God?

Tuesday
of the Seventh Week of Easter

(Eternal life is this:
to know you, the only true God,
and him whom you have sent, Jesus Christ.)
(John 17:3)

God is our creator. Jesus is our redeemer, true God and true man. The Spirit is our sanctifier. Everything else in our tradition comes from knowing God, our creator, redeemer, and sanctifier. This is the foundation of the entire creed and teachings of our church.

Jesus has entrusted this truth and his saving work to us by the power of the Spirit. Our faith means we live the life of the risen Christ that blossoms into hope and love. It also means that we share the gift with others, as Jesus shared it with others. It must be shared more by living than by preaching.

Prayer. Happy are we when we put our trust in God.

Reflection. Personal prayer is a key instrument of the Spirit to lead me into the life of God, so how am I praying these days?

Wednesday
of the Seventh Week of Easter

I consecrate myself for their sakes now,
that they may be consecrated in truth.
(John 17:19)

When someone or something is consecrated, it is set apart
for a special purpose. Jesus tells us that he is consecrated
so that we may be consecrated in truth. The truth is that we, the
people of God, are to carry on his mission. He came into the world
not to be of the world but to heal the world. We share in his healing
mission as a people and as individuals. Not only are we called, but
we are empowered by the Holy Spirit to live that call.

The church's primary role is to be in the world and to bring it to
Christ. Every Christian has a role. Children, elderly people, suffering
folks of all ages, teachers, volunteers, businesspeople, religious,
and clergy are consecrated by the Spirit to bring victory over sin
and death, to lead all nations to the resurrected Christ.

Prayer. God, be with me and with all my sisters and brothers
so that we may be missionaries wherever we are and in whatever
way we can be.

Reflection. My mission statement is this: . . .

Thursday
of the Seventh Week of Easter

I have given them the glory you gave me.
(John 17:22)

What is this glory that Jesus has given us? It is the mission to live our life as he lived his. Through Baptism and the gift of faith, we have been made other Christs. His objectives and values must be ours. We are glorified by the trust that Jesus has in us.

We are not told to go out on mission alone. Jesus sends his Spirit to support us. We can count on the Spirit to be with us as we establish unity among those who bear the name of Jesus and as we live the Good News before all people.

Prayer. "O God . . . / I have no good apart from you" (Psalm 16:1–2).

Reflection. If unity is a sign of God's presence, do I bring people together?

Friday
of the Seventh Week of Easter

"Simon, son of John, do you love me . . . ?" "Yes, Lord,"
Peter said, "you know that I love you." (John 21:15)

Years ago, some seminarians passed around a personnel
evaluation sheet to determine who Jesus should have
made the first leader of the Christian community. Peter showed up
furthest down on the list of good candidates. He was a poor fisher-
man. He betrayed Jesus three times. He was obviously insecure in
his faith.

However, because God's ways are not our ways, Jesus questions
Peter, "Do you love me?" Three times Peter replies, "You know that I
love you." Jesus concludes, "Feed my sheep." Scared, impulsive Peter
is chosen to be the head shepherd because he loves Jesus. Love
is not one of many values sought by God. It is the *central* value.
Without it we are nothing. The Scriptures, the sacraments, the
community, devotions, prayer, and fasting are all fruitless without
love. The material the Spirit used to make us to the image and
likeness of God is love.

Prayer. God, you know I love you.

Reflection. If Christians loving one another is the true test of
my faith, what's the state of my loving?

Saturday
of the Seventh Week of Easter

Your business is to follow me. (John 21:22)

God's expression in flowers, birds, trees, animals, land-scapes, and human beings reveals variety and beauty. The Trinity itself seems to attest to God's preference for unity *with* diversity. The struggle for global unity must be marked by a deep reverence for other cultures. Local churches have to have arms wide enough to make all feel at home in their embrace. Truth does not have to be sacrificed to achieve unity. Nor should orthodoxy be used as an excuse for slavish control.

The business of all of us is to follow Christ. No matter if we are fat or thin, Asian or African, a farmer or a chemist, a woman or a man, all of us are equally and mutually called to follow together in the great multiplicity of uniquenesses, one in Christ's business.

Prayer. May we be one as the Trinity is one.

Reflection. I am unique and everyone else is unique. How can we walk together?

Pentecost Sunday

Receive the Holy Spirit.
(John 20:22)

The Jewish feast of Pentecost was celebrated fifty days after Passover. People came from all over to celebrate God's Covenant with Israel. The disciples huddled in the Upper Room, afraid, waiting as they were told to do. Suddenly, with a great wind and tongues of fire, the Holy Spirit descended on them as promised by Jesus. The church was born.

These motley Apostles were now completely new persons. They spoke out boldly and clearly. People of various nationalities heard the message in their own tongues and were converted. The Spirit was creating a powerful new community. It would have many gifts and ministries given for the common good. Jesus promised the Spirit would come with power, the power to give freedom of heart. His promise was fulfilled. This power is still with us today, urging us to act justly, love tenderly, and walk humbly with our God.

Prayer. God, send out your spirit and renew the face of the earth.

Reflection. Am I filled with the Holy Spirit, renewing and fashioning me?

"Monsignor Chiara has written a gem of daily reflections for the journey through Lent, the Easter season, and Pentecost. The reflections are based in the challenges of contemporary life, but they come from wisdom of experience and prayer. This is not a book to read. This is a book to pray." **Msgr. Jim McNamara,** pastor of Our Lady of Grace Church and author of *The Power of Compassion* and *In the Presence of the Wise and Gentle Christ.*

"Monsignor Chiara's positive, gentle, yet challenging approach will encourage us to journey with Jesus in freedom and joy! These reflections are a clear call to each of us to consider what Lent, Easter, and Pentecost are truly about: contemplation leading to action. They inspire us to deepen our relationship with Jesus by becoming aware of his action in our lives." **Leonore Toscano, OP,** director of the Opening Word Program in Amityville, New York